CAMBRIDGE LIBRARY COLLECTION

Books of enduring scholarly value

Religion

For centuries, scripture and theology were the focus of prodigious amounts of scholarship and publishing, dominated in the English-speaking world by the work of Protestant Christians. Enlightenment philosophy and science, anthropology, ethnology and the colonial experience all brought new perspectives, lively debates and heated controversies to the study of religion and its role in the world, many of which continue to this day. This series explores the editing and interpretation of religious texts, the history of religious ideas and institutions, and not least the encounter between religion and science.

Memoirs of the Late Rev. John Wesley

This three-volume account of the life of John Wesley (1703–91) was published in the year of his death. Written by John Hampson (*c.*1753–1819), a Church of England clergyman and former Methodist preacher, the work also contains a thorough review of Wesley's writings and a history of Methodism. Hampson's excellent overview of contemporary assessments of the preacher is more balanced than John Whitehead's two-volume *Life of the Rev. John Wesley* (1793–6), which has also been reissued in this series. Volume 1 explores Wesley's lineage and early life, including his journey to America in 1735 and his conversion in 1738. This volume also contains short chapters on his brothers Samuel and Charles. Drawing on a wide range of sources, the work remains important for its informed appraisal of this religious movement and its founder.

T0370885

Cambridge University Press has long been a pioneer in the reissuing of out-of-print titles from its own backlist, producing digital reprints of books that are still sought after by scholars and students but could not be reprinted economically using traditional technology. The Cambridge Library Collection extends this activity to a wider range of books which are still of importance to researchers and professionals, either for the source material they contain, or as landmarks in the history of their academic discipline.

Drawing from the world-renowned collections in the Cambridge University Library and other partner libraries, and guided by the advice of experts in each subject area, Cambridge University Press is using state-of-the-art scanning machines in its own Printing House to capture the content of each book selected for inclusion. The files are processed to give a consistently clear, crisp image, and the books finished to the high quality standard for which the Press is recognised around the world. The latest print-on-demand technology ensures that the books will remain available indefinitely, and that orders for single or multiple copies can quickly be supplied.

The Cambridge Library Collection brings back to life books of enduring scholarly value (including out-of-copyright works originally issued by other publishers) across a wide range of disciplines in the humanities and social sciences and in science and technology.

Memoirs of the Late Rev. John Wesley

With a Review of His Life and Writings,
and a History of Methodism,
from its Commencement in 1729,
to the Present Time

VOLUME 1

JOHN HAMPSON

CAMBRIDGE
UNIVERSITY PRESS

CAMBRIDGE
UNIVERSITY PRESS

University Printing House, Cambridge, CB2 8BS, United Kingdom

Published in the United States of America by Cambridge University Press, New York

Cambridge University Press is part of the University of Cambridge.
It furthers the University's mission by disseminating knowledge in the pursuit of
education, learning and research at the highest international levels of excellence.

www.cambridge.org
Information on this title: www.cambridge.org/9781108064187

This edition first published 1791
This digitally printed version 2013

ISBN 978-1-108-06418-7 Paperback

MEMOIRS

OF THE LATE

Rev. JOHN WESLEY, A. M.

WITH A REVIEW OF HIS

LIFE and WRITINGS,

AND A

HISTORY of METHODISM,

From it's Commeneement in 1729, to the prefent time.

By JOHN HAMPSON, A. B.

, ὃ δε ανεξέιαςος βιος, δ βιωῖος ανθρωπω. PLATO.

VOL. I.

SUNDERLAND:

PRINTED FOR THE AUTHOR,

BY JAMES GRAHAM; AND SOLD BY J. JOHNSON,
ST. PAUL'S CHURCH-YARD, LONDON.

M.DCC.XCI.

PREFACE.

THE subjects of which they treat, the characters of the principal agents, and the just claims of the public to be made acquainted with the actions and opinions of remarkable persons, are sufficient authorities for the appearance of these memoirs.

For some reasons, of which it is not necessary to inform our readers, as well as others, which it may be proper to mention, the author had long determined, at a fit opportunity, to write the life of Mr Wesley. It was more than probable, such a life would not be overlooked. Some one would be certain to undertake

a

it: and confidering the colour of his
moft intimate connections, and the
unlimited deference, with which, in
this circle, it has been the fafhion to
regard him, a danger was apprehended, left the public fhould be
misinformed, either by the fuppref-
fion of fome important facts, or by
a partial and inaccurate relation.

    This apprehenfion was a power-
ful incentive to the prefent work;
and occafioned an adventure not
wholly deftitute of difficulty or of
danger. There muft neceffarily be
a degree of difficulty in the deline-
ation of characters replete with light
and fhade; diftinguifhed by great
virtues, and fullied by ftrange
peculiarities : and there is always
fome danger, that is, fome *critical*
danger in the difcuffion of topics,

(iii)

in which fo many, from different principles, are interefted.

To paint fuch portraits to the life, and yet generally to pleafe, were too arduous a tafk. But nothing can be an excufe for mifreprefentation. All that can, or ought to be done in fuch a cafe, is to draw a likenefs, not flatteringly difgufting, nor ex-aggerated to deformity, but as near-ly as poffible, a juft tranfcript of truth and nature. And this, with whatever fuccefs, is attempted in the following fheets.

It could anfwer no valuable pur-pofe, to inform the public of the tedious labours of hunting for in-formation through a variety of pu-blications, in which a continual famenefs of incidents, and confe-quently of fentiment and expref-

fion, and the neceffity of tracing
dates, thinly fcattered through a
multitude of pages, confiderably increafed the difficulty. It is of more
importance to acquaint them, that
the authorities referred to in the
narrative, are Mr Wefley's writings
in general, particularly the fermons,
the journals, and his controverfial
pieces : and laft, though not leaft,
is a correfpondence between the family of the Wefleys and others, from
1724 to 1739, which had lain neglect-
ed for many years, and was communicated by a grandchild of Mr
Samuel Wefley to Mr Badcock, by
him to a literary friend, and by this
gentleman to a near relation of the
Author; who begs leave to add, that
all this had been infufficient for his
purpofe, had he not long cultivated

an acquaintance with the writings and principles of Mr Wefley and his affociates. He alfo acknowledges his obligations for much information concerning the elder branches of the family, to the fprightly and entertaining remarks of a gentleman already mentioned, which were publifhed fome years ago in Maty's Review, and the Weftminfter Magazine.

The only circumftance which feems to demand an apology, is the publication of thefe memoirs during Mr Wefley's life. Was he a mere private gentleman, whatever might be his diftinction in the republic of letters, fuch an apology might be neceffary. But his cafe is peculiar. He has been for more than half a century, in the moft ex-

tenfive import of the word, a public
character. It is impoffible to make
him more fo, than he has rendered
himfelf.

There is yet another confideration. In the following pages,
fome of his fingularities are dif-
cuffed with a degree of freedom,
but it is hoped alfo, with impartiality and candour. It may be
queftioned, whether there ever was
a man of fenfe, even in his own
connexion, who thought him incapable of mifconduct or of error. If
there be fuch, no one is obliged to
follow his example. The Author of
thefe memoirs certainly does not.
He never was infenfible to the virtues of Mr Wefley; nor is he ignor-
ant of his foibles. And fince years
have not blunted his faculties *;

* See preface to fermons publifhed in 1788.

since the hand of time, in scattering his hoary honours upon his head has in no respect impaired his understanding, these pages are submitted, with the greater confidence to his censure and the public inspection. Should they contain errors, if he will point them out, they shall be rescinded. Should there be any circumstance, in which his character is misrepresented, or the truth in any respect violated, it certainly has been occasioned, not by prejudice or malevolence, but involuntary misapprehension, which in some instances is but too much the portion of human nature. Whenever any thing of this kind shall be detected, an explicit acknowledgment and recantation shall be made. By this means, every mistake of any consequence will be rectified; the public will be in poſſeſſion of more cor-rect information; and a preciſe view of his genius and tranſactions will be preſented to poſterity.

Such are the motives which gave riſe to this publication. Of the va-lidity of the one, and the execution of the other, the public will decide: and to that deciſion it is chearfully ſubmitted. A perſon, who with his uſual *modeſty*, chuſes to ſtile himſelf a *friend* of Mr Weſley, is ſaid to have demanded, who "could have the audacioufnefs to write a life of Mr Weſley while he was yet alive?" If he will look into the title-page, that will inform him.

From what has been ſaid, it will appear that theſe memoirs were in-tended for publication during Mr

Wefley's life. Since the former part of this preface was written, he is no more. But we fee no reafon to withold them. Eminent characters ought to be delineated and examined : and we know nothing more ufeful or more important to mankind, than a faithful reprefentation of the foibles and excellencies of public perfons.

Vol. I.   b

CONTENTS of VOL. I.

M E M O I R S

OF THE

REV. JOHN WESLEY, A. M.

———————————

C H A P. I.

Miscellaneous Articles relative to the Family.

THE ardour for biographical information was perhaps never so great
as in the present age. In such a period
no apology can be deemed necessary, for
attempting the history of a man, so eminent and distinguished as the subject of
these memoirs. The singular manner
in which he was first introduced to the
notice of the public; the peculiarity of
his character; and the authority he so

A

long maintained over a numerous and rapidly-increasing sect, must render an accurate review of such a life a valuable acquisition.

The author of these memoirs is afraid to flatter either his readers or himself with promises of absolute impartiality. He wishes indeed to arrive at this distinction, and is determined to attempt it: but such is the force of particular prepossessions, and so few writers of history or biography have succeeded in this most essential circumstance, that he trembles for himself, and is checked by a just anxiety, lest he should fall into a too general error, and become subject to the common condemnation.

The character of this gentleman is so eccentric, and so peculiarly has he been distinguished, by his situation, from the rest of mankind, that it is impossible ei-

ther to fpeak or to think of him, within
the ufual limits of moderation. As none
ever judged of Luther or Calvin, or
any head of a party, as they would of
more private charaĉters; fo it muſt be
with Mr Wefley. His friends and admi-
rers will doubtlefs confider him as an
apoſtle, and rank him with the moſt
diſtinguiſhed perfons of the primitive
times; while his enemies, who probably
conſtitute the more numerous body, will
not fail to regard him as a hypocrite, or
an enthufiaſt. Some will perhaps go yet
farther; and, by a ſtrange combination,
unite thefe charaĉters together.

The family, from which he is defcend-
ed, will be better known to poſterity,
from his own charaĉter, and from the
feĉt, of which he is the founder, than
from the genius and abilities of his an-
ceſtors. His grandfather, John Wefley,

was a minifter among the Non-conform-
ifts; and in the reign of Charles II. became involved in the calamities of the
times, and was ejected, by the act of
uniformity, from a living, which he held,
near Blandford in Dorfetfhire. 'At the
age of twenty-five, he officiated as a
preacher, without ordination, having only
an appointment to his office by a particular congregation; and it is moft probable, that he never was ordained to a
cure of fouls. A curious dialogue, on
this fubject, between this gentleman and
the then Bifhop of Briftol, is preferved
by Calamy, and is alfo inferted by Mr
Wefley, in one of his Journals. It evin-
ces confiderable piety on his part, with no
fmall degree of fhrewdnefs; while the
Bifhop's candour and moderation certainly do him the higheft honour.

The fon of this Mr Wefley was called

(5)

Samuel. While his father lived, he was
probably educated in the principles of
non-conformity, and fpent fome time at
one of their academies; but his father
dying when he was very young, and not
having had time to imbibe the fentiments
of the party, he entered himfelf at Exeter College, Oxford, where he was admitted to his degrees in the ufual courfe,
and taking holy orders, was firft prefented to the living of Epworth, and afterwards to that of Wroote, in Lincolnfhire.

Mr Samuel Wefley married the youngeft daughter of Dr Samuel Annefley, who
was a celebrated Non-conformift, and
firft coufin to the Earl of Anglefey. Dr
Annefley was an excellent man, and in
great efteem among his brethren; and
was ejeded from the living of St. Giles's,
Cripplegate, in 1662.

Mr Wefley, during his refidence at

(6)

Oxford, imbibed the ſtrongeſt prejudi-
cies againſt Diſſenters of every deſcription; repeatedly laſhed them from the
pulpit and the preſs; and exerted every
effort of ridicule and argument, to render
them contemptible. His zeal exceeded
his liberality: but in thoſe days every
thing was carried to an unwarrantable
exceſs; and it is certain that, in the decline of life, he abated much of this warm
and intolerant ſpirit, and piouſly applied
himſelf to the duties of his profeſſion.

The principles of non-conformity have
been generally conſidered, by the members of the eſtabliſhment, as unfavour-
able to monarchy. Many of the diſſenters
of thoſe days were decidedly ſo; and this
diſpoſition, which had been long cultivated, by the political pamphlets, during
the civil wars, and under the protectorate,
was ſtill cheriſhed in private, by meet-

ings, in which politics were united with conviviality; and the enthusiasm of the moment frequently hurried the company into the utmost rage of indecency and extravagance. One of these was the Calve's Head Club. The name is sufficiently expressive of the intention of the meeting; while the toasts, which they drank, and the conversation, that took place on such occasions, were republican and daring in the highest degree. One of their songs, which was composed for the 30th of January, may be cited as a specimen, and perhaps not the worst that might be produced, both of the wit and the spirit of the party.

'THE AXE IS LAID TO THE ROOT, &c.'

" 'Twas an action great and daring,
 Nature smil'd at what they did ;
When our fathers, nothing fearing,
 Made the haughty tyrant bleed.

A 3

Priefts and we, this day obferving,
   Only differ in one thing;
They are canting, whining, ftarving;
   We, in raptures, drink and fing.

Advance the emblem * of the action,
   Fill the calf-fkin full of wine;
Drinking ne'er was counted faction;
   Men and gods adore the vine."

Thefe " hellifh rhymes," as they have
been juftly called, breathe a fpirit equally
favage and vindictive. Whatever were
the faults of Charles, they were more
than compenfated by his misfortunes.
Educated, as he faid to his parliament, at
the feet of Gamaliel, it is no wonder that
he fell into fo abfurd a conduct, or that
fuch a conduct fhould produce fo fatal a
cataftrophe. James, with much pedantry
and affectation of learning, had a narrow
and contracted mind, and was, in truth,
neither a man nor a monarch. He uni-

* The axe.

ted the utmoſt contempt for the people
with the higheſt poſſible idea of the divine
right and prerogative of kings : ſo that
his own want of reſolution, and the ſpirit
of the times, could alone prevent him
from becoming a moſt furious tyrant.
Under ſuch a preceptor, his ſon imbibed
thoſe principles, which, if carried to their
extent, muſt have overturned the conſti-
tution, and at laſt brought him to the
block. But the inſults offered to fallen
majeſty were unworthy a great and enlightened people. They were juſtly abhorred by the majority of the nation,
and Mr Weſley's oppoſition to ſuch proceedings, reflects no diſhonour upon his
memory.

It is remarkable, that this gentleman,
in an early edition of the Dunciad, was
involved in the ſame cenſure with Dr
Watts; the former, a rigid churchman,

and the latter, the firſt name among the
diſſenters. But the injury was ſoon re-
repaired, by a handſome and juſt compliment from the poet; for Mr Weſley and
Dr Watts were, at leaſt, as excellent cha-
raꞓters as any in the kingdom.

The paſſage, here alluded to, is in the
deſcription of the library of the goddeſs,
in the firſt book :

" Here all his ſuff'ring brotherhood retire,
" And 'ſcape the martyrdom of jakes and fire;
" A Gothic library—of Greece and Rome
" Well purg'd, and worthy Settle, Banks and
       Broome."

Theſe names are inſerted inſtead of Weſley and Watts; and it is not improbable,
that this alteration may be aſcribed,
among other reaſons, to the friendſhip of
the poet for the younger Mr Samuel
Weſley, and to a mild, but ſpirited re-
monſtrance of Dr Watts, who pointed

out to Pope the injuſtice of ſuch unme-
rited ſatire.

This amiable Doctor ſometimes ſuffer-
ed in his public, when he muſt have
been beloved in his perſonal capacity ;
and ſeveral of the wits of that time, who
would have ſpared the man, did not fail
to laſh the diſſenter. In the Satires of
Dr Young, there is a ſevere and moſt un-
juſt reflection on his intimacy with Mrs
Rowe :

" Iſaac, a brother of the canting ſtrain,
" When he has knock'd at his own ſkull in vain,
" To beauteous Marcia often will repair,
" With a dark text, to light it at the fair.
" O how his pious ſoul exults, to find
" Such love for holy men in woman kind !
" Pleas'd with her learning, with what rapture he
" Hangs on her bloom, like an induſtrious bee,
" Hums round about her; and with all his power,
" Extracts ſweet wiſdom from ſo fair a flower."

Thus it is, that even the beſt men, of
different parties, tilt at one another. But

the fatyrist fhould have recollected, that
dullnefs had no part in Dr Watts; and
that, though an amiable man might very
properly cultivate the friendfhip of an
accomplifhed woman, it is impoffible that
he fhould learn divinity from Mrs Rowe,
or from any woman in the world. This
country has produced few characters fuperior to Dr Watts.

Mr Wefley was a voluminous writer.
He was the author of a Latin Comment
on Job; a work of much erudition, and
perhaps, for that reafon, but little read.
But it is furely more worthy of perufal,
than many publications, which the wit-
lings of the day have extolled to the
fkies. He alfo wrote the Hiftory of the
Bible, and the Life of Chrift, in verfe,
with feveral fmaller pieces. His larger
poems were rather injurious, than advantageous to his reputation; and, in-

ftead of increafing his eftimation with the
public, expofed him to the derifion of
the wits, and the cenfure of the critics.
But none treated him with more feverity,
than the author of the Difpenfary, in the
following lines :

" Had Wefley never aim'd in verfe to pleafe,
" We had not rank'd him with our Ogilvies;
" Still cenfures will on dull pretenders fall,
" A Codrus fhould expect a Juvenal."

Mr Wefley was by no means infenfible
of the force of the fatire; and there is
ftill extant a copy of verfes, in which he
has retaliated upon Garth, with great
fpirit, for the compliment he fo modeftly
pays himfelf. Two lines have been cited,
which are full in point :

" Who wonders, he fhould Weffey Codrus call,
" Who dares furname himfelf a Juvenal?"

Garth feems indeed to have been upon
excellent terms with himfelf, and does

not appear to have made the proper al-
lowances, in Mr Wefley's café, for the
difficulty of the undertaking. Of the
many, who have written on extenfive fubjects from fcripture, fcarcely any have
fucceeded. Mr Wefley certainly did not;
and I know but one that did. His
fon Samuel, who was really a poet, while
he takes notice of his father's piety, acknowledges that he failed. He perifhed
in too great an attempt :

" He fung how God, the Saviour, deign'd t'expire,
" With Vida's piety, tho' not his fire."

And it may be obferved, without any reflection on the merit of Garth, that, had
he written a life of Chrift, he certainly
had loft the fame, which he acquired by
his Difpenfary. One may go ftill farther:
had he written equally well on each occafion, he would not have been equally
fuccefsful, in the opinion of the critics. So

great is the difference in the fubjects!

But, notwithftanding his want of fuccefs, in this fpecies of compofition, Mr
Wefley was by no means a defpicable
poet. There are feveral of his fmaller
pieces, which are excellent; efpecially
the Hymn of Eupolis to the Creator.
Perhaps I may be fingular; but it has always ftruck me as one of the beft pieces,
in this kind of meafure, in the Englifh
language; and I could never read it,
without fuch feelings as very few poems
have been able to produce. That the
reader may judge for himfelf, and, by
way of compenfation to the much inju-
red memory of a worthy man, it is here
inferted, as it ftands in the firft volume
of the Arminian Magazine.

THE OCCASION.

PART OF A (NEW) DIALOGUE BETWEEN
PLATO AND EUPOLIS.

(THE REST NOT EXTANT.)

EUP. But is it not a little hard, that you ſhould baniſh all our fraternity from your new commonwealth? What hurt has father Homer done, that you diſmiſs him among the reſt?

PLATO: Certainly the blind old gentleman lyes with the beſt grace in the world. But a lye handſomely told, debauches the taſte and morals of a people. Beſides, his tales of the gods are intolerable, and derogate, in the higheſt degree, from the dignity of the divine nature.

EUP. But do you really think theſe faults inſeparable from poetry? May not the one ſupreme be ſung without any intermixture of them?

PLATO. I muſt own, I hardly ever ſaw any thing of that nature. But I ſhall be glad to ſee you, or any other, attempt and ſucceed in it. On that condition, I will gladly exempt you from the fate of your brother poets.

EUP. I am far from pretending to be a ſtandard; but I will do the beſt I can.

THE HYMN.

" Author of being, ſource of light,
With unfading beauties bright,
Fulneſs, goodneſs, rolling round
Thy own fair orb, without a bound:
Whether thee thy ſuppliants call,
Truth or good, or one, or all,
Ei or Iao; thee we hail,
Eſſence, that can never fail,
Grecian or Barbaric name,
Thy ſtedfaſt being, ſtill the ſame.
Thee, when morning greets the ſkies,
With roſy cheeks and humid eyes;
Thee, when ſweet declining day
Sinks in purple waves away;

B

Thee will I fing, O Parent Jove,
And teach the world to praife and love.
   Yonder azure vault on high,
Yonder blue, low, liquid fky,
Earth, on it's firm bafis plac'd,
And with circling waves embrac'd,
All-creating power confefs,
All their mighty maker blefs.
Thou fhak'ft all nature with thy nod;
Sea, earth, and air confefs the God:
Yet does thy powerful hand fuftain,
Both earth and heaven, both firm and main.
   Scarce can our daring thoughts arife,
To thy pavilion in the fkies;
Nor can Plato's felf declare
The blifs, the joy, the rapture there.
Barren above thou doft not reign,
But circled with a glorious train,
The fons of God, the fons of light,
Ever joying in thy fight:
(For thee their filver harps are ftrung)
Ever beauteous, ever young,
Angelic forms their voices raife,
And through heav'ns arch refound thy praife.

The feather'd fouls, that fwim the air,
And bathe in liquid ether there,
The lark, precentor of their choir,
Leading them higher ftill, and higher,
Liften and learn ; th' angelic notes
Repeating in their warbling throats;
And ere to foft repofe they go,
Teach them to their lords below :
On the green turf, their moffy neft,
The evening anthem fwells their breaft :
Thus, like thy golden chain from high,
Thy praife unites the earth and fky.

Source of light, thou bidft the fun
On his burning axles run ;
The ftars, like duft, around him fly,
And ftrew the area of the fky.
He drives fo fwift his race above,
Mortals can't perceive him move :
So fmooth his courfe, oblique or ftrait,
Olympus fhakes not with his weight.

As the queen of folemn night,
Fills, at his vafe, her orb of light,
Imparted luftre ; thus we fee
The folar virtue fhines by thee.

Eirefione we'll no more,
Imaginary power, adore ;
Since oil and wool, and chearful wine,
And life fuftaining bread are thine.

 Thy herbage, O great Pan, fuftains
The flocks, that graze our attic plains ;
The olive, with frefh verdure crown'd,
Rifes, pregnant, from the ground ;
At thy command, it fhoots and fprings,
And a thoufand bleffings brings.
Minerva, only is thy mind,
Wifdom and bounty to mankind.
The fragrant thyme, the bloomy rofe,
Herb, and flower, and fhrub, that grows
On Theffalian Tempe's plain,
Or where the rich Sabeans reign,
That treat the tafte, or fmell, or fight,
For food, for med'cine, or delight ;
Planted by thy parent care,
Spring, and fmile, and flourifh there.
 O ye nurfes of foft dreams!
Reedy brooks, and winding ftreams,
Or murm'ring o'er the pebbles fheen,
Or fliding through the meadows green,

Or where thro' matted fedge you creep,
Trav'ling to your parent deep ;
Sound his praife, by whom you rofe,
That fea, which neither ebbs nor flows.

　　O ye immortal woods and groves !
Which the enamour'd ftudent loves,
Beneath whofe venerable fhade,
For thought and friendly converfe made,
Fam'd Hecadem, old hero, lies,
Whofe fhrine is fhaded from the fkies,
And thro' the gloom of filent night,
Projects, from far, it's trembling light ;
You, whofe roots defcend as low,
As high in air your branches grow,
Your leafy arms to heav'n extend,
Bend your heads, in homage bend ;
Cedars and pines, that wave above,
And the oak, belov'd of Jove.

　　Omen, monfter, prodigy,
Or nothing are, or Jove, from thee !
Whether various nature play,
Or reinvers'd, thy will obey,
And to rebel man declare,
Famine, plague, and wafteful war.

Laugh, ye profane, who dare defpife
The threat'ning vengeance of the fkies,
Whilft the pious, on his guard,
Undifmay'd, is ftill prepar'd :
Life or death, his mind's at reft,
Since what thou fend'ft, muft needs be beft.
No evil can from thee proceed,
'Tis only fuffer'd, not decreed;
Darknefs is not from the fun,
Nor mount the fhades, till he is gone;
Then does night obfcene arife,
From Erebus, and fill the fkies,
Fantaftic forms the air invade,
Daughters of nothing, and of fhade.

   Can we forget thy guardian care,
Slow to punifh, prone to fpare!
Thou brak'ft the haughty Perfian's pride,
That dar'd old Ocean's power deride.
Their fhipwrecks ftrew'd th' Eubean wave;
At Marathon they found a grave.
O ye bleft Greeks! who there expir'd,
For Greece, with pious ardour fir'd,
What fhrines or altars fhall we raife,
To fecure your endlefs praife?

Or need we monuments fupply,
To refcue what can never die ?
    And yet a greater hero far,
(Unlefs great Socrates could err)
Shall rife to blefs fome future day,
And teach to live, and teach to pray.
Come, unknown inftructor, come !
Our leaping hearts fhall make thee room :
Thou, with Jove, our vows fhalt fhare,
Of Jove and thee we are the care.
    O Father King! whofe heav'nly face
Shines ferene on all thy race,
We thy magnificence adore,
And thy well-known aid implore :
Nor vainly for thy help we call,
Nor can we want ; for thou art all."

Such is the piece I have ventured to
commend. It's beauties are numerous
and ftriking ; and I am perfuaded that
no reader of tafte and difcernment will
object to it's introduction : the lefs fo,
when it is confidered, that though many
B 4

have heard of this gentleman's name in
the Dunciad and the Difpenfary, but few
are acquainted with his claims to a more
honourable diftinction. Had all the imi-
tators and tranflators of the ancients
done them equal juftice, they would
have no reafon to repine at being feen
in an Englifh drefs. But Mr Wefley's
talents as a writer are the leaft of his
praife. He was not merely a man of
learning and ability. His piety and integrity were ftriking and exemplary.
He was given to hofpitality; and in every refpect a moft excellent parifh prieft :
and after a long and ufeful life, died at
Epworth, in April, 1735. The truly
Chriftian refignation, the fortitude and
magnanimity which crowned the laft moments of this valuable man, were fo ftriking, and are fo admirably defcribed in
a letter from his fon, the late Mr Charles

Wefley, to his brother Samuel, that it
were an injury to the public to omit it.

" Dear Brother,

After all your defire of feeing
my father alive, you are at laft affured,
you muft fee his face no more, till he is
raifed in incoruption. You have reafon
to envy us, who could attend him in the
laft ftage of his illnefs. The few words
he could utter I faved, and I hope, fhall
never forget them. Some of them were,
" Nothing too much to fuffer for heaven.
The weaker I am in body, the ftronger
and more fenfible fupport I feel from
God. There is but a ftep between me
and death. To morrow I would fee you
all with me round the table, that we may
once more drink of the cup of blefling,
before we ' drink it new in the kingdom
of God.' With defire have I defired to

eat this paffover with you before I die."

The morning he was to communicate, he was fo weak and full of pain, that he could not, without the utmoft difficulty, receive the elements; often repeating, " thou fhakeft me; thou fhakeft me;" but immediately after receiving, there followed the moft fenfible alteration : he appeared full of peace and faith, which extended even to his body; for he was fo much better, that we almoft hoped he would recover. The fear of death he had entirely conquered, and at laft gave up his lateft human defires, of finifhing Job*, paying his debts, and feeing you.

He often laid his hand upon my head, and faid, " Be fteady. The Chrift-ian faith will furely revive in this king-dom. You fhall fee it, though I fhall not." To my fifter Emily he faid,

* A Latin commentary on that book.

" Don't be concerned at my death.
God will then begin to manifeſt himſelf
to my family." When we were met a-
bout him, his uſual expreſſion was, "Now
let me hear you talk of heaven." On
my aſking him whether he did not find
himſelf worſe, he replied, " Oh! my
Charles, I feel a great deal : God chaſt-
ens me with ſtrong pain; but I praiſe
him for it ; I thank him for it ; I love
him for it."

On the 25th, his voice failed him, and
nature ſeemed exhauſted; when, on my
brother's aſking him whether he was not
near heaven, he anſwered diſtinſtly, and
with the moſt of hope and triumph that
could be expreſſed in ſounds, " Yes, I
am." He ſpoke once more, juſt after
my brother had uſed the commendatory
prayer. His laſt words were, " Now
you have done all." This was about

half paſt ſix. From this time till ſun-ſet, he made ſigns of offering up himſelf, till my brother, having again uſed the pray-er, the very moment it was finiſhed, he expired. His paſſage was ſo ſmooth and infenſible, that notwithſtanding the ſtop-ping of his pulſe, and the ceaſing of all ſigns of life and motion, we continued over him a conſiderable time, in doubt whether the ſoul was departed or no. My mother, who for ſeveral days before he died, hardly ever entered his cham-ber, but ſhe was carried out in a fit, was far leſs ſhocked at the news than we ex-pected ; and told us, that now ſhe was heard, in his having ſo eaſy a death, and in her being ſtrengthened to bear it."

Such was the death of this venerable clergyman. And it is no exaggeration to ſay, that a better man, or a more vi-gilant and faithful paſtor he certainly

did not leave behind him. He united
the zeal and courage of a martyr with
the fimplicity and evangelical fpirit of an
apoftle; and though he had no great
caufe to boaft the munificence, he poffeffed the efteem of fome of the firft characters in the nation :

" Her gracious fmiles not pious Anne denied,
" And beauteous Mary bleft him, when fhe died."

The Dean of St. Patrick's, who was an
acute difcerner of merit, bore ample teftimony to his worth. It is faid, that he
was ftrongly folicited, by the emiffaries
of James II. to countenance the mea-
fures of the court, in favour of popery ;
and that his complaifance to the monarch
would have been acknowledged, by confiderable preferment. But he abfolutely
refufed to read the declaration; and,
though furrounded by foldiers and in-
formers, juftified that refufal, by a bold

and pointed difcourfe from Daniel iii.
17. 18. " If it be fo, our God, whom we
ferve, is able to deliver us from the burning, fiery furnace, and he will deliver us
out of thine hand, O king! But if not, be
it known unto thee, O king! that we will
not ferve thy gods, nor worfhip the gold-
en image, which thou haft fet up."

He was a laborious and ufeful preacher. His converfation was folid and entertaining, his carriage affable and cour-
teous, and his beneficence much fuperior
to his income. We need not however
confider him as a faultlefs character. His
undue warmth againft the diffenters, in
early life, has been already noticed;
nor can it be concealed, that both he
and feveral of the family were remarkable for fuch high notions of prerogative
and authority, both in church and ftate,
as feem fcarcely compatible with the con-

ftitution of this country. Yet it is certain that he was one of the firft, if not
the firft writer in defence of the revolu-
tion; a circumftance which can fcarcely
be accounted for, but by fuppofing that
whiggifm was, in his opinion, more to-
lerable than popery; and that, to prevent
the eftablifhment of the latter, the former
might be endured.

His wife, Mrs Sufannah Wefley, was
a lady of great merit and accomplifh-
ments; and united the graces of her own
fex with the judgment and fortitude of
the other. She brought him nineteen
children; feveral of whom grew up to
maturity, and were diftinguifhed by their
talents. It is faid of one, who afterwards
married a Mr Wright, that, at eight years
of age, fhe was well acquainted with the
Greek Teftament, and could repeat a
confiderable part of it. This lady does

not appear to have been happy in her connections. Whatever was the caufe, fhe feems to have fallen a prey to the feverity of her fate; and, if we can credit the following epitaph, which fhe compofed for herfelf, actually died of a broken heart:

" Deftin'd while living to fuftain
An equal fhare of grief and pain;
All various ills of human race,
Within this breaft had once a place.
Without complaint fhe learnt to bear
A living death, a long defpair.
Till hard oppreft by adverfe fate,
O'ercharg'd fhe funk beneath it's weight,
And to this peaceful tomb retir'd,
So much efteem'd, fo long defir'd;
The painful, mortal conflict's o'er;
A broken heart can bleed no more.

The fimplicity and pathetic air of thefe lines is a fufficient proof, that her diftrefs was not imaginary; and I believe fhe died at an early period. Several compofitions,

by the fame hand, have appeared in
different publications; and though fad-
dened by an air of tender melancholy,
in general but too vifible, difcover an
elegant and enlightened mind. I fhall
only add the following addrefs to her
dying infant :

" Tender foftnefs ! infant mild !
Perfect, fweeteft, lovelieft child.!
Tranfient luftre ! beauteous clay !
Smiling wonder of a day !
Ere the laft convulfive ftart
Rends thy unrefifting heart ;
Ere the long enduring fwoon
Weigh thy precious eye-lids down ;
Ah ! regard a mother's moan ;
Anguifh deeper than thy own !
    Faireft eyes, whofe dawning light
Late with rapture bleft my fight ;
Ere your orbs extinguifh'd be,
Bend their trembling beams on me.
Drooping fweetnefs ! verdant flower !
Blooming, with'ring in an hour !

C

Ere thy gentle breaſt ſuſtains
Lateſt, fierceſt, mortal pains,
Hear a ſuppliant ; let me be
Partner in thy deſtiny."

Another ſiſter was addreſſed by a clergyman, whoſe name was H*ll, and who
was introduced to the family, by Mr John
Weſley, in one of his excurſions from the
univerſity to Epworth. It is a painful
taſk, on ſome occaſions, to ſpeak what
we know to be the truth; and it muſt
always be ſo, to a man of feeling and
benevolence, when it affects the moral
character of thoſe, who have lately quit-
ted the theatre of human life. But as
this gentleman's conduct was public and
notorious, and more eſpecially, as Mr
Badcock, in the Weſtminſter Magazine,
and Mr Weſley, in ſeveral paſſages of his
Journals, have given the public much in-

formation on this subject, it will scarcely be deemed uncharitable or impertinent, if I should take notice of the faults of a man, so intimately connected with the family. It seems too, that a distinction is to be observed. There are some foibles, which are to be ascribed to the infirmity of human nature. In such cases, censure must degenerate into detraction. But, in instances of actual vice, and those too of the most alarming and pernicious tendency, the rule, that we should not speak ill of the dead, can hardly be observed; and their faults ought to be censured, not merely, that we may form an accurate estimation of their real character, but as a proper admonition to others.

Mr H*ll paid his addresses to Miss Kezzy Wesley. It appears, from the intimations scattered up and down the

C 2

letters and other papers, in which he is mentioned, that, in perfon and under, ftanding, and in every refpeft, but pro, bity and virtue, he was formed to cap- tivate the fex. The young lady, and the reft of the family, who confidered the offer as highly advantageous, gave him a favourable reception; and, for fome time, the confent of his mother was the only obftacle to the match. But it was not long before he deferted the younger, in favour of her elder fifter; and, the better to accomplifh his purpofe, had recourfe to the old fubterfuge of hypo- crify, under the mafk of piety, and pre- tended a revelation, that it was the will of heaven. The dictates of honour and confcience, the interpofition of every branch of the family, and every thing that could be urged, was ineffectual. The marriage was celebrated; and Mr

Badcock fays (what feems more wonder
ful than all the reft) that the lady he had
deferted, attended him and her fifter to
his curacy in Wales.

After fuch a beginning, it will be no
matter of furprife, that he prefently grew
diffatisfied with his wife, and, having em-
braced polygamy in principle, carried it
as far as he could, into practice, and
ftrongly recommended it in converfation
and in his public difcourfes.

It feems rather remarkable, that the
opportunity of intimate acquaintance and
obfervation was not fufficient, to prevent
John and Charles from being duped, by
the artifices of this fpecious man. They
regarded him, for a confiderable time,
as a Chriftian of the firft order; and it
appears, to the laft moment of his life,
to have been the opinion of Mr John
Wefley, that, when he firft knew him,

he was fincere in his religion. But his
egregious hypocrify, in fome future
fcenes, renders this at leaft highly pro-
blematical: and it is much to be lamented, that a man, to whom nature had been
fo lavifh of her favours, fhould fo grofsly
have difhonoured himfelf, and done fo
much injury to others.

Mr Samuel Wefley, however, was not
to be deceived by appearances. He was
too acute an obferver, too refined a ftudent in men and manners, to give credit
to his pretentions to fuperior fanctity;
and, in a letter to John, gave his judgment, concerning him, in thefe remark-
ble terms : " I am fure, I may well fay
of that marriage, it will not, cannot come
to good. I never liked the man, from
the firft time I faw him. His fmooth-
nefs never fuited my roughnefs. He appeared always to dread me as a wit and

a jefter, like Rivington. This, with me, is a fure fign of guilt and hypocrify. He never could meet my eye in full light. Confcious that there was fomething foul at bottom, he was afraid I fhould fee it, if I looked keenly into his eye. Charles fends me a bad account indeed. If you will allow Kezzy what was propofed, I will take her with me. Thus fhe will be delivered from difcontent, perhaps, or a worfe paffion."

But the intentions of this excellent brother were fruftrated. The defection of a man, who had engaged her tendereft affections, was a fhock, to her peace, too rude to be fupported; and involved her in a melancholy, that preyed upon her conftitution, and, in a little time, brought her to the grave. The unhappy man was for many years, the fport of the moft unruly paffions: and his adven-

tures, in England and in foreign countries, were as various and eccentric, as
was his own character. Sometimes he
acted as a medical man, and sometimes
as a clergyman; and, with equal ease,
exhibited in canonicals, or figured away
with his sword and cane, and scarlet
cloak. At length, having deserted his
wife, and run off with his maid; having
played a thousand freaks, and escaped a
thousand dangers, he returned home, and
was seen officiating in a church in London, where, not long before his death,
he delivered an extemporary discourse
from the first verse of the 19th psalm,
which a gentleman, who heard it, says,
was inimitably elegant and pathetic. He
was a man of great learning and ingenuity; and it is said that, in his latter
end, he gave full proof of contrition,
and died in peace.

CHAP. II.

Of SAMUEL WESLEY the Younger.

THIS gentleman was the eldeſt ſon
of Samuel and Suſannah Weſley,
and was born, at Epworth, about the
year 1690. He was educated at Weſtminſter ſchool, and from thence elected
to Chriſt Church. In both theſe places,
ſo deſervedly eminent for polite learning,
he diſtinguiſhed himſelf by his compoſitions, and acquired the reputation of an
excellent claſſic. His ſkill in the languages and ſcienes was accurate and extenfive; and, having taken the degree of
Maſter of Arts, he was ſent for, to offici-

ate as an ufher at Weftminfter. Not long after, under the aufpices of the celebrated Dr Atterbury, then Dean of Weftminfter, he took orders; and was univerfally efteemed, as an able preacher and a judicious divine. A diftinguifhed excellence of Mr Wefley, was his benevolence. He was humane and charitable, both by nature and from principle, and indefatigable in the fervice of the indigent. What he was incapable of alone, he frequently accomplifhed, by his influence upon others. Among other things of this kind, we are informed, that the firft infirmary at Weftminfter was much forwarded, both in the defign and execution, by his induftrious charity.

He was held in high eftimation, by fome of the moft diftinguifhed characters of the day. Oxford, Atterbury, and

Pope were his particular friends; and it
appears by a letter from the laſt of theſe,
that he procured him ſeveral ſubſcribers
to a volume of poems which he publiſh-
ed. It is certain however, that he derived no ſolid advantage from theſe connections. On the contrary, they ruined
his profpects in the church, and equally
prevented his advancement in the ſchool.
Walpole became his moſt inveterate enemy : while he, provoked by the part this
Palinurus took againſt him, retaliated,
without mercy, on Sir Robert, and vent-
ed his indignation in a thouſand jeſts and
paſquinades; which, though they ſtung
the miniſter to the quick, did not fail,
at the ſame time, to confirm him in his
reſolution, that Mr Weſley ſhould never
riſe at Weſtminſter. The animoſity between them was mutual; and yet, ſuch
was the filial piety of this high-ſpirited

man, that, in the latter end of his father's
life, who was but in narrow circumftances, he even condefcended, in his favour,
to folicit a minifter, he both hated and
defpifed. The folicitation did not fucceed.

The banifhment of Atterbury maae no
difference in Mr Wefley's attachment. His
integrity was inflexible. The Bifhop of
Rochefter, whofe political principles were
congenial to his own, and whofe talents
were of the firft order, he had always
been accuftomed to regard, with the moft
refpectful veneration: and, under all the
obloquy of attainder and deprivation, he
did not difcontinue his attentions. He
made no diftinction between the Prelate,
in the heighth of honour and pofperity,
and the fame perfon arraigned before the
lords, and fentenced to perpetual exile.
He honoured the memory of his patron

with a pathetic elegy ; and he had paid
the fame tribute, on the death of his
Lordſhip's daughter, Mrs Morrice. A
circumſtance with which the Biſhop was
ſo ſenſibly affeĉted, as to declare, that if
ever he returned home with honour, Mr
Weſley ſhould find it. But the Biſhop
did not return ; and his friend, after
preſiding a few years at a grammar ſchool
at Tiverton, in Devon, died in November, 1739, and in the forty-ninth year
of his age.

He was the author of a volume of
poems in quarto, on a variety of ſubjeĉts;
ſome grave and religious ; ſome ludicrous
and ſatyrical. But, in general, they have
the beſt tendency, and are calculated,
either to correĉt ſome vice, or to incul-
cate ſome branch of morality and virtue.
They abound with marks of profound
erudition, great obſervation and know-

ledge of mankind, with a moſt lively and
vigorous imagination. His fire was however ſuperior to his correctneſs. His
verſes, in many parts, poſſeſs not that
harmony they might have acquired, had
he taken more pains to poliſh and refine
them. But they are maſculine and nervous in the higheſt degree. Dean Swift
greatly admired the Battle of the Sexes;
which I think he republiſhed in Dublin;
and of which, for this reaſon, ſome ſup-
poſed him to be the author. Some of
his hymns are very fine. His tales, for
the eaſy and agreeable humour they contain, merit a particular attention. He
has very nearly approached, if he did not
equal Prior, whom he took for his mo-
del. The ſatire of theſe ingenious pieces,
though exquiſitely pointed, is facetious
and well-tempered: and they are full of
admirable inſtructions, for the comfort

and regulation of life. But perhaps the
very beſt, though one of the ſhorteſt
of his compoſitions, is the following paraphraſe on a verſe of Iſaiah :

" The morning flowers diſplay their ſweets,
    And gay their ſilken leaves unfold ;
As careleſs of the noon-day heats,
    And fearleſs of the evening cold.

Nipt by the wind's unkindly blaſt,
    Parch'd by the ſun's directer ray,
The momentary glories waſte,
    The ſhort-liv'd beauties die away.

So blooms the human face divine,
    When youth it's pride of beauty ſhews ;
Fairer than ſpring the colours ſhine,
    And ſweeter than the virgin roſe.

Or worn by ſlowly rolling years,
    Or broke by ſickneſs in a day,
The fading glory diſappears,
    The ſhort-liv'd beauties die away.

Yet theſe, new riſing from the tomb,
    With luſtre brighter far ſhall ſhine,

Revive, with ever-during bloom,
  Safe from difeafes and decline.

Let ficknefs blaft, and death devour,
  Since heav'n muft recompenfe our pains;
Perifh the grafs, and fade the flower,
  Since firm the word of God remains."

Among the papers Mr Wefley left behind him, is the following letter; which,
while it fhews the terms upon which he
was with the Earl of Oxford, informs us
alfo of his intention of publifhing notes
on Hudibras. It is dated from Dover-
ftreet, Auguft 7. 1734, and is as follows:

" Rev. Sir,

  I am forry and afhamed to fay
it; but the truth muft come out, that I
have a letter of your's, dated June the
8th; and this is the 7th of Auguft, and
I have but now fet pen to paper, to anfwer it.

I affure you, that I was very glad to hear
from you, and fince, that you are much
mended in your health. Change of air
will certainly be of great fervice to you;
and I hope you will ufe fome other exer-
cife, than that of the fchool.   I hear you
have had an increafe of above forty boys,
fince you have been down there.   I am
very glad, for your fake, that you are fo
well approved of.   I hope it will, in every refpeft, anfwer your expeftation : if
your health be eftablifhed, I make no
doubt, but thofe parts will be to your
mind; which will be a great pleafure
to me.

There is very little news ftirring.
They all agree, that the Bifhop of Wor-
cefter is dying.   They fay Hoadley is to
fucceed him, and Potter Hoadley; but
how farther I cannot tell; nor does the
town pretend, which is a wonderful thing!

D

I am very glad you was induced to read over Hudibras three times, with care. I find you are perfectly of my mind, that it much wants notes; and that it will be a great work. Certainly it will be so, to do it as it should be. I do not know any one so capable of doing it as yourself. I speak this very sincerely. Lilly's life I have; and any books, that I have, you shall see, and have the perusal of them, and any other part, that I can assist. I own I am very fond of the work; and it would be of excellent use and entertainment.

The news you read in the papers, of a match between my daughter and the Duke of Portland, was completed at Marybone chapel. I think there is the greatest prospect of happiness to them both. I think it must be mutual. One part cannot be happy without the other.

(51)

Here is great harmony of temper, and a liking to each other; which is, I think, a true foundation for happinefs. Compliments from all here attend you.

I am, Sir,

Your moſt affectionate

humble fervant,

OXFORD.

P. S. The two boys are well. Pray, let me hear from you foon; and let me know, under your own hand, how you do."

His Lordſhip was certainly right. The genius of Mr Weſley; his knowledge of the tranfactions of thofe times; and, let me add too, his extreme averfion and contempt for the Oliverian fanatics, rendered him the fitteſt perfon in the world for a commentator on fuch a writer: and notwithſtanding the induſtry and abi-

D 2

lity of Mr Grey, who is faid to have had many of his notes, it is to be lamented, as a real lofs to the republic of letters, that this propofal was not carried into execution.

The modefty of the poet was ftriking and uncommon. He informs the public, in an advertifement prefixed to his poems, that they were publifhed, not from " any opinion of excellency in the verfes themfelves;" but merely on account of " the profit propofed by the fubfcription." There are not many writers, who, with equal talents, are poffeffed of equal diffidence; and after fuch a declaration, every one will be pleafed to hear, that the fubfcription was fuch, as to make up a confiderable part of a decent competency, which he left for the fupport of his widow and daughter. This daughter, who was his only child, mar-

ried Mr Earle, a furgeon, at Barnftaple, by
whom fhe had a daughter, who married
a Mr Manfell of Dublin.

This article cannot be more properly
clofed, than by fubjoining the infcription
on his tomb-ftone, in the church-yard,
at Tiverton.

Here lie, interred,
the Remains of the Rev. SAMUEL WESLEY, A. M.
fometime Student of Chrift-church, Oxon :
a man, for his uncommon wit and learning,
for the benevolence of his temper,
and fimplicity of his manners,
defervedly beloved and efteemed by all.
An excellent Preacher :
but whofe beft fermon
was the conftant example of an edifying life.
So continually and zealoufly employed
in acts of beneficence and charity
that he truly followed
His bleffed Mafter's example,
in going about, doing good.

D 3

Of fuch fcrupulous integrity,
that he declined occafions of advancement in the world,
thro' fear of being involved in dangerous compliances,
and avoided the ufual ways to preferment
as ftudioufly as many others feek them.
Therefore, after a life fpent
in the laborious employment of teaching youth,
firft, for near twenty years,
as one of the Ufhers in Weftminfter fchool;
afterwards, for feven years,
as Head-mafter of the free fchool, at Tiverton,
he refigned his foul to God,
Nov. 6. 1739, in the 49th year of his age.

C H A P. III.

Of Charles Wesley, A. M.

CHARLES, the third fon, was born
at Epworth, in 1708. He received his education at Weftminfter, and
was thence elected to Chrift-church,
where he proceeded A. M. It is faid,
that he was born in the feventh month
of his mother's pregnancy; and though
he did not enjoy the ftrength and firm
conftitution of his brothers, he lived to
a good old age. He was an excellent
fcholar, and had he engaged in the
higher walks of verfe, would certainly
have been efteemed a confiderable poet.
He confined himfelf chiefly however to
hymn writing : and it is to be lamented

D 4

that he did fo, though many of his pieces
are, without difpute, among the beft
things in that fpecies of compofition.
This gentleman was of a warm and lively
difpofition, of great franknefs and integrity; and there was an honefty in his
nature, which fome would perhaps call
precipitancy and imprudence; and which
would not fuffer him to pafs over, or
to bear with any thing his judgment
difapproved. He had a great regard
for men of principle in all perfuafions;
and, with all his heart, abhorred a hypocrite, and the whole tribe of fyco-
phants and flatterers: nor could' perfons
of fuch a character, be long in his prefence with impunity. His converfation
was pleafing and inftructive, and often
feafoned with wit and humour. His
religion of the right fort; not gloomy
and cynical; but cheerful and benevo-

lent: and whatever might have been the cafe in his youth, in his latter days he was certainly no enthusiast.

In April 1749, he married Mifs Eleanor Gwynne, a moft amiable lady, of Garth, in Brecknockfhire, who brought him two fons and a daughter, now living. The fons are much known and admired for their mufical talents. The younger, a few years ago, became a convert to popery; and I am authorifed to fay, that this event was one of the greateft afflictions of Mr Wefley's life. The light, in which he confidered it, cannot be better reprefented, than by obferving, that one of the laft reflections that fell from his lips, was a declaration, that he forgave the perfon. by whofe means this converfion was brought about.

As Mr Charles was of a more retired temper than his brother, and lefs expofed to public obfervation; and as he rather concurred with him in what he directed, than acted of himfelf, little can be faid of him as a public character. In 1734 he wrote to his brother Samuel, informing him of the intended marriage, between one of his fifters and Mr H ll. We have already feen, that this match was broken off; and that the gentleman in queftion married her elder fifter. Some time previous to this marriage, and not long before his father's death, Charles wrote his fifter Martha the following epiftle; from which it appears, that the poet was as much miftaken in her, as he had been in her whimfical inamorato; and that the lady, though affifted by every confideration of piety and juftice, and urged by fo nervous and pathetic a reprefentation, was not proof againft the blandifhments of an artful and accomplifhed man:

TO MISS MARTHA WESLEY.

When want and pain, and death befiege our gate,
And every folemn moment teems with fate,
While clouds and darknefs fill the fpace between,
Perplex th' event, and fhade the folded fcene,
In humble filence wait th' unutter'd voice,
Sufpend thy will, and check thy forward choice;
Yet wifely fearful, for th' event prepare,
And learn the dictates of a brother's care.
How fierce thy conflict, how fevere thy flight!
When hell affails the foremoft fons of light !
When he, who long in virtue's paths hath trod,
Deaf to the voice of confcience and of God,
Drops the fair mafk, proves traitor to his vow,
And thou the temptrefs, and the tempted thou !
Prepare thee then to meet th' infernal war,
And dare beyond what woman knows to dare;
Guard each avenue to thy flutt'ring heart,
And act the fifter's and the Chriftian's part.
Heav'n is the guard of virtue ; fcorn to yield,
When fcreen'd by Heav'ns impenetrable fhield :
Secure in this, defy th' impending ftorm,
Tho' Satan tempt thee in an angel's form.

And oh! I fee the fiery trial near:
I fee the faint, in all his forms, appear!
By nature, by religion taught to pleafe,
With conqueft flufh'd, and obftinate to prefs,
He lifts his virtues in the caufe of hell,
Heav'n, with celeftial arms, prefumes t' affail,
To veil, with femblance fair, the fiend within,
And make his God fubfervient to his fin!
Trembling, I hear his horrid vows renew'd,
I fee him come, by Delia's groans purfued;
Poor injur'd Delia! all her groans are vain;
Or he denies, or lift'ning, mocks her pain.
What tho' her eyes with ceafelefs tears o'erflow,
Her bofom heave with agonizing woe!
What tho' the horror of his falfehood near,
Tear up her faith, and plunge her in defpair!
Yet, can he think (fo blind to heav'ns decree,
And the fure fate of curs'd apoftacy)
Soon as he tells the fecret of his breaft,
And puts the angel off, and ftands confeft;
When love, and grief, and fhame, and anguifh meet,
To make his crimes, and Delia's wrongs complete,
That then the injur'd maid will ceafe to grieve,
Behold him in a fifter's arms—and live?

Miftaken wretch! by thy unkindnefs hurl'd,
From eafe, from love, from thee, and from the world,
Soon muft fhe land on that immortal fhore,
Where falfehood never can torment her more;
There all her fuff'rings, all her forrows ceafe,
Nor faints turn devils there, to vex her peace.
Yet hope not then, all fpecious as thou art,
To taint, with impious vows, her fifter's heart;
With proffer'd worlds, her honeft foul to move,
Or tempt her virtue to inceftuous love.
No! wert thou as thou waft! did heav'ns firft rays
Beam on thy foul, and all the godhead blaze!
Sooner fhall fweet oblivion fet us free
From friendfhip, love, thy perfidy and thee:
Sooner fhall light in league with darknefs join, ⎤
Virtue and vice, and heav'n with hell combine, ⎬
Than her pure foul confent to mix with thine; ⎦
To fhare thy fin, adopt thy perjury,
And damn herfelf, to be reveng'd on thee;
To load her confcience with a fifter's blood,
The guilt of inceft, and the curfe of God!"

As this is one of his earlieft productions, we may alfo pronounce it (fome
of his hymns excepted) confiderably the

beſt. It is written *con amore :* and it is
eaſy to ſee, that his whole heart was engaged in it. Many other pieces, ſuch as
the elegies on the death of Whitfield and
Jones; the addreſs to his brother John,
and ſeveral more, which were compoſed
haſtily, and on particular occaſions, are
ſo much inferior to this little poem, that
they ſcarcely appear to come from the
ſame hand. It is perhaps not eaſy to
aſſign the cauſe; but there ſeems a kind
of fatality to attend poems on religious
ſubjects : and whatever may be the reaſon, the fact is notorious, that not one
in twenty is worth reading.

Mr Charles Weſley was ſubject, during his whole life, to a certain inſtinctive
fear of dying, from an apprehenſion he
could never conquer, that he muſt ſuffer ſomething terrible in his laſt moments. This idea was frequently preſent

to his imagination, and had fuch an effect upon his mind, that, in his laft illnefs, he conftantly defired thofe, who vifited him, to pray that God would grant him patience and an eafy death. His fears were happily difappointed. The frame was fairly worn out ; and, after a gra-dual and general decay, he departed with the utmoft ferenity and compofure, and exchanged this life, for a better, in March 1788, and in the eightieth year of his age.

Notwithftanding his connection with Methodifm, he was always attached to the church of England, and gave orders, on his death-bed, that his remains fhould be interred, not in his brother's burying ground at the City Road, becaufe it was not confecrated; but in the church-yard at Mary bone, the parifh in which he had fpent the laft years of his life. Some

will perhaps read this remark with a fmile
of difdain, while others will regard it
with approbation: but let the former
remember, that, if this was a weaknefs
in Mr Wefley, it was at leaft a pardon-
able weaknefs; and had it's origin in
fome of the beft principles of human
nature. The writer of thefe pages had
a great efteem for this amiable man;
and with pleafure takes this opportunity
of paying a tribute to a memory, which
he will never ceafe to refpect and to regret. He quits, with reluctance, a fubject that will ever be pleafing to his re-
collection; but begs leave firft to prefent the reader with a beautiful portrait
of his humanity and benevolence, in a
poetical comment on that much difputed
paffage, in which the fpirit of Samuel
predicts to Saul, " by this time to-morrow thou and thy fons fhall be with me."

" What can thefe folemn lines portend?
Some gleam of hope, when life fhall end.
Thou and thy fons, though flain, fhall be
To-morrow in repofe with me :
Not in a ftate of hellifh pain,
If Saul with Samuel remain;
Not in a ftate of damn'd defpair,
If loving Jonathan be there."

E

C H A P. IV.

Of John Wesley, A. M.

MR JOHN WESLEY, whofe life and actions are the chief fubject of thefe memoirs, was the fecond fon of Samuel and Sufannah Wefley; and was born at Epworth, in Lincolnfhire, according to his own account on the 21ft of June, 1703; though according to that of one of his parents, and of the perfon who was his nurfe, in 1700. But there is the moft pofitive proof that his own date is the true one. An incident of a particular nature took place in the family, which occafioned the abfence of his father from home, and his feparation from

Mrs Wefley for upwards of a year and a half. During this time, King William died, and Queen Anne came to the throne. On her acceffion, Mr Wefley returned to Epworth; and Mr John Wefley was the firft child after that meeting.

The difference in thefe accounts arofe from an event which happened when he was about fix years old, and was very near proving fatal to him. The parfonage houfe at Epworth, by fome accident, took fire, and was burnt to the ground; and with it the parifh regifter. The memory of his efcape, on this occafion, is preferved in one of the early prints of him; in which, under the head, is a reprefentation of a houfe in flames, with a motto, " Is not this a brand plucked out " of the burning ?" There is alfo a letter from his mother, to a clergyman in the neighbourhood, containing a parti:-

cular account of the whole tranſaction.
The letter is as follows, and is dated
Auguſt 24th, 1709.

" On Wedneſday night, February the
9th, between the hours of eleven and
twelve, ſome ſparks fell from the roof of
our houſe, upon one of the children's (Het-
ty's) feet. She immediately ran to our
chamber, and called us. Mr Weſley,
hearing a cry of fire in the ſtreet, ſtarted
up ; (as I was very ill, he lay in a ſepa-
rate room from me) and opening his
door, found the fire was in his own houſe.
He immediately came to my room, and
bid me and my two eldeſt daughters riſe
quickly and ſhift for ourſelves. Then he
ran and burſt open the nurſery door, and
called to the maid, to bring out the children. The two little ones lay in the bed
with her ; the three others in another

bed. She fnatched up the youngeft, and
bid the reft follow; which the three elder
did. When we were got into the hall,
and were furrounded with flames, Mr
Wefley found he had left the keys of the
doors above ftairs. He ran up and recovered them, a minute before the ftair-
cafe took fire. When we opened the
ftreet door, the ftrong north-eaft wind
drove the flames in with fuch violence,
that none could ftand againft them. But
fome of our children got through the
windows, and the reft through a little
door into the garden. I was not in a
condition to climb up to the windows;
neither could I get to the garden door. I
endeavoured three times to force my paffage through the ftreet door, but was as
often beat back by the fury of the flames.
In this diftrefs, I befought our bleffed
Saviour for help, and then waded thro'

the fire, naked as I was, which did me
no farther harm, than a little fcorching
my hands and my face.

When Mr. Wefley had feen the other
children fafe, he heard the child in the
nurfery cry. He attempted to go up the
ftairs, but they were all on fire, and would
not bear his weight. Finding it impoffible to give any help, he kneeled down
in the hall, and recommended the fcul
of the child to God."

[This child was John. The reft muft
be given in his own words.]

" I believe it was juft at that time I
waked ; for I did not cry, as they ima-
gined, unlefs it was afterwards. I remember all the circumftances as diftinctly as
though it were but yefterday. Seeing
the room was very light, I called to the
maid to take me up. But none anfwering,
I put my head out of the curtains, and

faw ftreaks of fire on the top of the room.
I got up and ran to the door, but could
get no farther, all the floor beyond it being in a blaze. I then climbed up on a
cheft, which ftood near the window:
one in the yard faw me, and propofed
running to fetch a ladder. Another anfwered, ' There will not be time; but I
have thought of another expedient. Here
I will fix myfelf againft the wall: lift a
light man, and fet him on my fhoulders.'
They did fo, and he took me out of the
window. Juft then the whole roof fell
in; but it fell inward, or we had all been
crufhed at once. When they brought
me into the houfe, where my father was,
he cried out, ' Come, neighbours! let
' us kneel down! let us give thanks to
God! he has given me all my eight children: let the houfe go: I am rich enough!'

E 4

The next day, as he was walking in the garden, and furveying the ruins of the houfe, he picked up part of a leaf of his Polyglot Bible, on which juft thofe words were legible, " Vade; vende omnia quæ habes, et attolle crucem et fequere me." Go; fell all that thou haft; and take up thy crofs, and follow me!"

Mr Wefley, as well as the reft of the children, received the firft rudiments of learning from his mother, who appears to have been well qualified for the in-ftruction of youth, and whofe fuccefs was almoft without example. When any of the children were to learn their letters, fhe contrived, during that time, to have nothing elfe to do, and gave herfelf en-tirely to them. Samuel, who was the eld-eft, learnt his letters in a few hours. One or two of them, whom fhe thought very dull, were almoſt three days before they were perfeçt : but, in general, they were maſters of the alphabet in twenty-four hours, and in a few days could read a chapter in the Bible.

At an early age, John was removed to the Charter-houſe ; and from thence to Chriſt-church ; whence, having taken his firſt degree in arts, he was eleçted fellow of Lincoln in 1724, and proceeded to the degree of A. M. in 1726. His eleçtion to Lincoln ſeems to have been greatly promoted by his brother's intereſt in that ſociety : at leaſt this appears the moſt natural conſtruçtion of ſome expreſſions in a letter, in which he ſays, " I ſhould certainly have wrote you word of my ſuccefs on Friday ; (all Ihurſday I was detained at Lincoln ;) but that I thought it more adviſeable, ſince I had promiſed to ſend

fome verfes in a few days, to do both in
the fame letter. I am at the fame time
to afk pardon for letting any thing prevent my doing the firft fooner, and to return you my fincere and hearty thanks,
as well for the frefh inftance of affection
you now give me, in the pains you take
to qualify me for the enjoyment of that
fuccefs, which I owe chiefly, not to fay
wholly to your intereft. I am the more
ready to profefs my gratitude now, becaufe I may do it with lefs appearance of
defign than formerly; of any other defign
I hope, than of fhewing myfelf fenfible of
the obligation, and that in this refpect at
leaft, I am not unworthy of it."

Mr Wefley was foon regarded at Oxford as a man of talents, and his compofitions were always diftinguifhed by
peculiar excellence. He was a critic in
the learned languages, and his logical

fkill was eminently confpicuous. It is
faid, that at a very early period he puz-
zled every opponent by the fallacies of an
art, of which he was greatly enamoured;
and that with the gaiety, and perhaps a
fmall mixture of the vanity of youth, he
laughed at them for being fo eafily van-
quifhed.

His whole time however was by no
means taken up with the feverer ftudies.
He did not difdain to pay his court to the
mufes; and feveral juvenile compofitions,
which are as animated and fprightly, as
they are claffical and elegant, fhow that
it was not altogether without fuccefs.
Moft of his pieces that we have feen are
tranflations from the Latin. The fubjects indeed are fuch as, in his latter
years, he would certainly have difapproved : but though they fhow that he was
not infenfible to the fervour of youthful

paffion, they will not difcredit his memory. Thofe that follow are felected, becaufe they appear in fome original letters
to his brother Samuel.

FROM THE LATIN.

As o'er fair Cloe's rofy cheek
 Carelefs a little vagrant paft ;
With artful hand around his waift,
 A flender chain the virgin caft.

As Juno near her throne above
 Her fpangled birds delights to fee ;
As Venus has her fav'rite dove,
 Cloe fhall have her fav'rite flea.

Pleas'd with his chains, with nimble fteps
 He o'er her fnowy bofom ftray'd ;
Now on her panting breaft he leaps,
 Now hides between, his little head.

Leaving at length his old abode,
 He found, by thirft or fortune led,

Her fwelling lips, that brighter glow'd
   Than rofes in their native bed.

Cloe, your artful bands undo,
   Nor for your captive's fafety fear;
No artful bands are needful now,
   To keep the willing vagrant here.

While on that heaven 'tis given to ftay
   (Who would not wifh to be fo bleft?)
No force can drive him once away,
   Till death fhall feize his deftin'd breaft!

———————

IN IMITATION OF QUIS DESIDERIO SIT PUDOR, &c.
SENT TO A GENTLEMAN ON THE DEATH OF HIS
FATHER.

What fhame fhall ftop our flowing tears?
   What end fhall our juft forrows know?
Since heaven, relentlefs to our prayers,
   Has given the long deftructive blow.

Ye mufes, ftrike the founding ftring,
   In plaintive ftrains his lofs deplore,

And teach an artlefs voice to fing
   The great, the bounteous, now no more!

For him the wife and good fhall mourn,
   While late records his fame declare;
And oft as rolling years return,
   Shall pay his tomb a grateful tear.

Ah! what avail their plaints to thee?
   Ah! what avails his fame declar'd?
Thou blam'ft alas! the juft decree
   Whence virtue meets it's full reward.

Tho' fweeter founds adorn'd thy tongue
   Than Thracian Orpheus whilom play'd,
When lift'ning to the morning fong,
   Each tree bow'd down its leafy head:

Never, ah! never from the gloom
   Of unrelenting Pluto's fway,
Could the thin fhade again refume
   It's ancient tenement of clay.

Indulgent patience, heav'n born gueft!
   Thy healing wings around difplay;

Thou gently calm'ſt the ſtormy breaſt,
  And driv'ſt the tyrant grief away.

Corroding care and eating pain,
  By juſt degrees thy influence own;
And lovely, laſting peace again
  Reſumes her long-deſerted throne.

HORACE, LIB. I. ODE XIX.

The cruel queen of fierce deſires,
  While youth and wine aſſiſtants prove,
Renews my long-neglected fires,
  And melts again my mind to love.

On blooming Glycera I gaze,
  By too reſiſtleſs force oppreſt!
With fond delight my eye ſurveys
  The ſpotleſs marble of her breaſt.

In vain I ſtrive to break my chain;
  In vain I heave with anxious ſighs:
Her pleaſing coyneſs feeds my pain,
  And keeps the conqueſts of her eyes.

Impetuous tides of joy and pain
By turns my lab'ring bofom tear;
The queen of love, with all her train
Of hopes and fears, inhabits there.

No more the wand'ring Scythian's might,
From fofter themes my lyre fhall move;
No more the Parthian's wily flight:
My lyre fhall fing of nought but love.

Hafte, graffy altars let us rear;
Hafte, wreaths of fragrant myrtle twine;
With Arab fweets perfume the air,
And crown the whole with gen'rous wine.

While we the facred rites prepare,
The cruel queen of fierce defires
Will pierce, propitious to my prayer,
Th' obdurate maid with equal fires.

O D E XXII.

Integrity needs no defence;
The man who trufts to innocence,

Nor wants the darts Numidians throw,
Nor arrows of the Parthian bow.

Secure, o'er Lybia's fandy feas,
Or hoary Caucafus, he ftrays;
O'er regions fcarcely known to fame,
Wafh'd by Hydafpes' fabled ftream.

While void of cares, of nought afraid,
Late in the Sabine woods I ftray'd;
On Sylvia's lips, while pleas'd I fung,
How love and foft perfuafion hung

A rav'nous wolf, intent on food,
Rufh'd from the covert of the wood;
Yet dar'd not violate the grove,
Secur'd by innocence and love.

Nor Mauritania's fultry plain,
So large a favage does contain :
Nor e'er fo huge a monfter treads
Warlike Apulia's beechen fhades.

Place me where no revolving fun
Does o'er his radiant circle run;

F

Where clouds and damps alone appear,
And poifon the unwholefome year:

Place me in that effulgent day,
Beneath the fun's directer ray;
No change from it's fix'd place fhall move
The bafis of my lafting love.

There needs no panegyric of thefe fu-
gitive pieces. Their intrinfic merit is a
fufficient recommendation; and confidering that they are hafty productions, and
that little time was employed in the compofition, and ftill lefs in revifing and cor-
recting them, they may fafely be pro-
nounced excellent. In fome of his letters, notice is taken of five or fix other
copies of verfes, which he wrote about
his twenty-firft or twenty-fecond year.
One of thefe was a tranflation of part of
the fecond Georgic, and another was an
imitation of the fixty-fifth Pfalm.

If we can depend upon his own account, and there does not appear any reason to the contrary, Mr Wesley, who had
a pious education, with the advantage of
the best examples in the conduct of his
parents, had an early disposition to religion. Soon after his admission at Lincoln, he became more serious than usual;
and, in a letter to his brother Samuel, of
the 24th of April 1726, intimates his
dislike of that kind of poetry, which is
so generally cultivated in youth. Speak-
ing of some verses, which a gentleman
of Exeter college had promised to write
out for him, he says, " Yesterday I saw
them, though not much to my satisfac-
tion, as being all on very wrong subjects,
and turning chiefly on romantic notions
of love and gallantry." Of these the
following are inserted as a specimen:

F 2

" By a cool fountain's flow'ry fide
   The fair Celinda lay ;
Her looks increas'd the fummer's pride
   Her eyes the blaze of day.

Quick thro' the air, to this retreat,
   A bee induftrious flew ;
Prepar'd to rifle ev'ry fweet,
   Under the balmy dew.

Drawn by the fragrance of her breath,
   Her rofy lips he found ;
There, in full tranfport, fuck'd in death,
   And dropt upon the ground !

Enjoy, bleft bee, enjoy thy fate,
   Nor at thy fall repine ;
Each God would quit his blifsful ftate,
   To fhare a death like thine!"

In the fame letter there is a tranflation
of part of the 46th pfalm; but whether it
is to be afcribed to this gentleman or to
Mr Wefley, does not clearly appear.

PSALM XLVI.

On God fupreme our hope depends,
  Whofe omniprefent fight,
Ev'n to the pathlefs realms extends
  Of uncreated night.

Plung'd in th' abyfs of deep diſtrefs,
  To him we raife our cry;
His mercy bids our forrows ceafe,
  And fills our tongue with joy.

Tho' earth her ancient feat forfake,
  By pangs convulfive torn;
Tho' her felf-balanced fabric fhake,
  And ruin'd nature mourn;

Tho' hills be in the ocean loft,
  with all their fhaggy load:
No fear fhall e'er moleft the juft,
  Or fhake his truft in God.

What tho' th' ungovern'd, wild abyfs
  His fires tumultuous pours?

What tho' the watry legions rife,
    And lafh th' affrighted fhores ?

What tho' the trembling mountains nod,
    Nor fland the rolling war ?
Sion fecure enjoys the flood,
    Loud echoing from afar.

The God moft high on Sion's hill
    Has fix'd high his abode ;
Nor dare th' impetuous floods affail
    The city of our God.

Nations remote and realms unknown,
    In vain rejeĉt his fway ;
For lo Jehovah's voice is fhown,
    And earth fhall melt away.

Let war's devouring furges rife,
    And rage on every fide ;
The Lord of Hofts our refuge is,
    And Jacob's God our guide.

In the firſt volume of the Arminian
Magazine, there is a paraphraſe, by Mr
Weſley, of part of the civ. pſalm; and
ſuch is it's excellence, that it would be
wrong to omit it.

Upborn aloft on ventrous wing,
  While ſpurning earthly themes I ſoar,.
Thro' paths untrod before,
What God, what Seraph ſhall I ſing?
Whom but Thee ſhould I proclaim,
Author of this wondrous frame?
  Eternal, uncreated LORD,
  Enſhrin'd in glory's radiant blaze!
At whoſe prolific voice, whoſe potent word,
Commanded Nothing ſwift retir'd, and worlds began
    their race..

Thou, brooding o'er the realms of night,
  Th' unbottom'd, infinite abyſs,
Bad'ſt the deep her rage ſurceaſe,
And ſaid'ſt, Let there be light!
  Ætherial light thy call obey'd,
Thro' the wide void her living waters paſt,

Glad fhe left her native fhade,
Darknefs turn'd his murmuring head,
Refigned the reins, and trembling fled;
The chryftal waves roll'd on, and fill'd the ambi-
    ent wafte.

In light, effulgent robe, array'd,
    Thou left'ft the beauteous realms of day;
The golden towers inclin'd their head,
    As their fovereign took his way.
The all-incircling bounds (a fhining train,
Miniftering flames around him flew)
Thro' the vaft profound he drew,
    When, lo! fequacious to his fruitful hand,
Heaven o'er th' uncoloured void, her azure cur-
    tain threw.

Lo! marching o'er the empty fpace,
    The fluid ftores in order rife,
With adamantine chains of liquid glafs,
    To bind the new-born fabric of the fkies.
Downward th' Almighty Builder rode,
Old chaos groan'd beneath the GOD,
    Sable clouds his pompous car,

Harneſt winds before him ran,
Proud to wear their maker's chain,
 And told, with hoarſe-reſounding voice, his
  coming from afar.

Embryon earth the ſignal knew,
And rear'd from night's dark womb her infant head;
Tho' yet prevailing waves his hills o'erſpread,
 And ſtain'd their ſickly face with pallid hue.
But when loud thunders the purſuit began,
Back the affrighted ſpoilers ran ;
 In vain aſpiring hills oppos'd their race,
O'er hills and vales with equal haſte,
The flying ſquadrons paſt,
 Till ſafe within the walls of their appointed place ;
There firmly fix'd, their ſure encloſures ſtand,
Unconquerable bounds of ever-during ſand!
He ſpake from the tall mountain's wounded ſide,
Freſh ſprings roll'd down their ſilver tide :
 O'er the glad vales, the ſhining wanderers ſtray,
Soft murmuring as they flow,
While in their cooling wave inclining low,
 The untaught natives of the field, their parch-
  ing thirſt allay.

High feated on the dancing fprays,
  Checquering with varied light their parent ftreams,
The feather'd quires, attune their artlefs lays,
  Safe from the dreaded heat of folar beams.

    Genial fhowers at his command,
    Pour plenty o'er the barren land:
    Labouring with parent throes,
    See! the teeming hills difclofe
    A new birth: fee chearful green,
    Tranfitory, pleafing fcene!
    O'er the fmiling landfkip glow,
    And gladden all the vale below.
    Along the mountain's craggy brow,
    Amiably dreadful now!
    See the clafping vine difpread
    Her gently rifing, verdant head;
    See the purple grape appear,
    Kind relict of human care!

Inftinct, with circling life, thy fkill
  Uprear'd the olive's loaded bough;
What time on Lebanon's proud hill,
  Slow rofe the ftately cedars brow.

Nor lefs rejoice the lowly plains,
   Of ufeful corn the fertile bed,
Than when the lordly cedar reigns,
   A beauteous, but a barren fhade.

While in his arms the painted train,·
   Warbling to the vocal grove,
Sweetly tell their pleafing pain, .
   Willing flaves to genial love.
While the wild-goats, an active throng;
   From rock to rock light-bounding fly
Jehovah's praife in folemn fong,
   Shall echo thro' the vaulted fky.

After much enquiry, we are not abfolutely certain at what time Mr Wefley
entered into holy orders ; all we know
is, that he was ordained in the year 1725,
by Dr Potter, afterwards Archbifhop of
Canterbury, and preached his firft fermon at Southlye, not far from Oxford,
where we find him again in 1771. There
is extant a correfpondence between feveral of the family on this fubject. The

firſt letter in this correſpondence is dated January 26th. It is addreſſed to
him by his father, and is diſtinguiſhed
by ſome judicious reflections on the ſa-
cred and important nature of the mini-
ſterial office. He ſuppoſes, that to deſire
to get into ſuch an office, like the ſons of
Eli, " to eat a piece of bread," though
it be the loweſt, is a motive not abſolute-
ly unwarrantable; that the deſire and intention to lead a ſtricter life is a ſtill better motive; but that the chief induce-
ments, and to which every thing elſe
ought to be ſubſervient, are " the glory
of God and the edification of our neighbour." Some men engage in the miniſtry, not only without any ſuch intentions, but with an averſion to the office:
and any one may perceive the propriety
of his obſervation on this caſe; " if a man
be unwilling and undeſirous to enter into

orders, tis eafy to guefs, whether he
fay, fo much as with common honefty,
that he trufts he is moved to it by the
Holy Ghoft." To young men he particularly recommends the Polyglot and
Grotius as the beft comments on fcripture, and concludes with an admonition
equally pertinent and affecting. " Work
and write while you can. You fee, Time
has fhaken me by the hand ; and Death
is but a little behind him. My eyes and
heart are now almoft all I have left: and
I thank God for them."

The fecond of thefe letters contains
fome excellent advice concerning moderation in youthful pleafures; and the third,
which is dated the 19th of October 1725,
and juft previous to the time when his
fon is fuppofed to have taken orders, is
intended to refolve fome doubts with regard to the Athanafian creed, and dif-

covers, if we miſtake not, equal moderation and ingenuity. But let the reader
judge for himſelf.

" You ſeem ſtaggered at the ſevere
words in the Athanaſian creed. Conſider,
their point is levelled againſt, and only
againſt obſtinate heretics. A diſtinction
is undoubtedly to be made, between what
is wilful, and what is in ſome meaſure
involuntary. God certainly will make a
difference. We don't ſo well know it.
We therefore muſt leave that to him, and
keep to the rule, which he has given us.

As to the main of the cauſe, the beſt
way to deal with our adverſaries, is to
turn the war and their own vaunted arms
againſt them. From balancing the
ſchemes, it will appear, that there are
many irreconcileable abſurdities and con-
tradictions in theirs; but none ſuch (tho'
indeed ſome difficulties) in ours. To in-

ſtance in one of a ſide. They can never prove a contradiction in our Three and One; unleſs we affirm them to be ſo in the ſame reſpect, which every child knows we do not. But we can prove there is one, in a creature's being a creator, which they affirm of our Lord:"

Theſe letters, from the elder Mr Weſley, are evidently written in anſwer to his ſon's queries on the ſubject; and they ſhow, on the one hand, ſuch ſolid piety, with ſo much rational affection; and on the other, ſuch conſcientiouſneſs and integrity, as reflect great honour on them both. It were indeed exceedingly to be wiſhed, that every father, eſpecially every clergyman, who intends his ſon for holy orders, were as capable of adviſing him, and every ſon diſpoſed to be as commendably ſerious and inquiſitive on ſo important a ſubject.

But, at the fame time that we exprefs our wifhes, we muft lament the impof-fibility of their accomplifhment. While young men, at the different feminaries, ftudy any thing but divinity, and read any books rather than the fcriptures; while they regard nothing in the church but her emoluments, and enter into or-ders upon exactly the fame principles, as they would enter into the army or the navy, fo long confcientioufnefs and inte-grity, either in taking orders, or in per-forming the ecclefiaftical duties, will be foreign to many of the candidates for the minifterial office. It is prefumed, none will be difpleafed with this comparifon. The intention is merely to intimate, that employments in the army or the navy are of a fecular, but thofe in the church of a fpiritual nature; and confequently, that none ought to engage in fuch an of

fice, without a fincere intention to promote piety in himfelf and others: and
no clergyman of real piety can be offended, becaufe he certainly is not included
in thefe reflections.

C H A P. V.

OF THE ORIGIN OF METHODISM.

WE have feen the principles on which Mr Wefley entered into holy orders. As he was not ordained to any cure, but as a fellow of his college, he refided there till the year 1735, having feveral pupils, and officiating as Greek lecturer and moderator of both the claffes. In this capacity, he difcover ed that love of ftrictnefs and difcipline, by which he has ever fince been diftinguifh ed. He was as vigilant over the morals of his pupils, as he was anxious for their improvement in literature ; and he ex pected from them an obedience which

we are authorized to fay, was without a
precedent in the univerfity. He required that they fhould rife very early in the
morning; that they fhould read no books
but fuch as he approved; and that in
their general conduct, and in every thing
that refpected their private ftudies, as
well as the ftatutable exercifes, they
fhould implicitly fubmit to his direc-
tions.

It is faid, and we are not difpofed to
doubt, that he was an excellent tutor.
His difcipline could fcarcely be without
it's ufe. The time of the young men
would be well filled up, which, at an
univerfity, is a principal thing: and
being totally excluded from gaming
and hunting, and a variety of other
amufements, not too friendly to learning, they could make the moft of the
advantages of that illuftrious feminary.

G 2

Every one knows, that fome of the firſt
charaĉters in the univerſe have been formed there; and that, with the previous
education at ſchool and a good capacity,
whoever reſides at college the uſual time,
muſt either be a man of learning or of
invincible indolence.

During his reſidence at Lincoln, Mr
Weſley became particularly ſerious and
religious; and ſeveral of his friends and
pupils, having the ſame diſpoſitions, they
formed into a kind of ſociety, which at
firſt, in November 1729, conſiſted of the
two Mr Weſleys, Mr Morgan of Chriſt-
church, and one more; into which were
admitted, ſome time after, Mr Clayton
of Brazen-noſe, Mr Hervey, Mr Whitefield, and ſeveral others. At firſt, they
read the claſſics every evening but Sunday, and on that day ſome book in divinity; but in a little time it is probable;

that their religious meetings were more frequent.

Mr Wefley afcribes his firft religious impreffions at Oxford to Bifhop Taylor's Rules for holy Living and Dying, which fell in his way; and thofe impreffions were confirmed and increafed by reading Stanhope's Kempis, and the Serious Call and Chriftian Perfection of Mr Law. In reading thefe books, he tells us, that he found fuch comfort as he had never felt before; and that, meeting with a religious friend, he began to alter " the form of his converfation, and to fet out in earneft upon a new life." He faw, as he obferves, more and more of the value of time; fhook off all his trifling acquaintance; applied himfelf more clofely to ftudy; watched againft actual fins, and advifed others to be religious, according to that fcheme of religion by

G 3

which he modelled his own life. In a
little time, fays he, " I was convinced
more than ever of the exceeding height
and breadth, and depth of the law of God.
The light flowed in fo mightily upon my
foul, that every thing appeared in a new
view. I cried to God for help, and re-
folved not to prolong the time of obey-
ing him, as I had never done before.
And by my continued endeavour to keep
his whole law, inward and outward, to
the beft of my power, I was perfuaded,
that I fhould be accepted of him, and that
I was even then in a ftate of falvation."

The fociety, with which he was connected, to an unufual ftrictnefs of deportment, and frequent meetings with
each other, foon added a more diffufive fcheme of utility. The principal
and moft active among them was Mr
Morgan. By his advice and example

they vifited the fick and the prifoners
in the caftle; they inftituted a fund for
the relief of the poor, and were fo dili-
gent in the ordinances of religion, and
fo induftrious in doing good, that they
began to be taken notice of, and were
prefently diftinguifhed by the name of
Methodifts, Sacramentarians, and the
Godly Club.

The better to accomplifh his benevo-
lent defigns, Mr Wefley abridged himfelf of all the fuperfluities, and of fome
things that are called the neceffaries of
life; and propofing their fcheme for the
relief of the poor to feveral gentlemen,
they increafed their fund to about eighty
pounds a year. Thefe things, added to
their obfervance of the fafts of the ancient church, and their ftrict attention to
every kind of religious duty, rendered
them, more and more obnoxious to cen-

fure; fo that they were now not only laughed at by the young men, but fome of the feniors of the univerfity began to interfere. One gentleman, a man of learning, and efteemed a man of piety, threatened his nephew, that, if he went any more to the weekly communion, he would turn him out of doors. The young gentleman however went as ufual. His uncle now fhook him by the throat, and threatened him to no purpofe; fo that, being difappointed in fuch methods, he changed his plan, and, by great mildnefs and condefcenfion, prevailed on him to abfent himfelf for at leaft five Sundays in fix, which he continued to do ever after.

In confequence of this, another gentleman prevailed on fome of the reft to promife, that they would receive the facrament only three times a year. It was now reported, that the college cenfors

were going to blow up the Godly Club
and Mr Wefley, perceiving the oppofition they would meet with, confulted his
father, and fome other gentlemen of piety and learning, whether they fhould retreat, or go forward. The anfwers were
fuch as they ought to be. They were
advifed to go on. The Bifhop of Oxford
and the officiating minifter at the Caftle
were confulted, who greatly approved
their proceedings : and indeed, unlefs a
man were a determined enemy to all religion, it was impoffible not to approve
them. The conduct of thefe young gentlemen did indeed appear ftrange, becaufe
fo contrary to the cuftoms of the place ;
but a voluntary fcheme, of fo much private and public good, fuch piety, with
fuch beneficence, certainly merited a different return : and if the univerfity in
general, inftead of ridiculing or perfecu-

ting them, had had the grace to imitate
their example, it would have been much
better both for the public and themfelves.

Mr Wefley's father was not likely to
give them any oppofition; for, when an
under-graduate at Oxford, he had obferved a fimilar conduct, having frequently vifited the prifoners at the Caftle. His
brother Samuel, who was never fufpected of enthufiafin, was of the fame mind;
which he declares in the ftrongeft terms
that could be employed on fuch an occafion. " I cannot fay (fays he) I thought you
always in every thing right; but I muft
now fay, rather than you and Charles
fhould give over your whole courfe, efpecially what relates to the Caftle, I would
chufe to follow either of you, nay both of
you to your graves. I cannot advife you
better, than in the words I propofed for a
motto to a pamphlet, " Stand thou fted-

fast as a beaten anvil; for it is the part
of a good champion to be flead alive and
to conquer."

Another clergyman, of known wifdom and integrity, was confulted on this
occafion. His anfwer was to the fame
purpofe; but there are fome expreffions
in it fo pointed and remarkable, that we
muſt infert them. " As to my own fenfe
of the matter, I confefs, I cannot but
heartily approve that ferious and religious turn of mind that prompts you and
your affociates to thofe pious and chari
table offices; and can have no notion of
that man's religion or concern for the
honour of the univerfity, that oppofes
you as far as your defign refpects the
colleges. I fhould be loth to fend a fon
of mine to any feminary, where his con-
verfing with virtuous young men, whofe
profeſt defign of meeting together, at

proper times, was to affift each other in forming good refolutions, and encouraging one another to execute them with conftancy and fteadinefs, was inconfiftent with any received maxims or rules of life among the members."

So far, it appears that they had conducted themfelves with equal piety and prudence. Some time in 1730 the fociety fuftained a fevere lofs in the deceafe of Mr Morgan, who was the firft promoter of it, and appears, from all accounts, to have been, in the ftricteft fenfe of the word, a gentleman and a chriftian. His piety was as enlightened as it was ardent: and as it may fafely be prefumed, that he does not now repent of his unwearied affiduity and zeal; fo, we can fee no reafon why he fhould be cenfured for them by others.

" Who blames the ftripling, for performing more
Than doctors grave, and prelates of three fcore?
Glad'ning the poor, where'er his fteps he turn'd,
Where pin'd the orphan, or the widow mourn'd;
Where pris'ners figh'd beneath guilt's horrid ftain,
The worft confinement and the heavieft chain!"

From Mr Wefley's firft journal we
learn, that the death of this young gentleman was charged to his and his brother's account; and it was faid, that the
rigorous abftinence which, by their advice, he had impofed on himfelf, had increafed his illnefs, and haftened his dif-
folution. To vindicate himfelf from this
charge, Mr Wefley wrote a long letter
to Mr Morgan's father, in which fome
will think he has effectually wiped off the
afperfion, by fhowing that, in 1730, Mr
Morgan had left off fafting about a year
and a half; whereas, at that time, Mr
Wefley had practifed it not quite half a
year. An elegy on Mr Morgan's death

is among the poems of Mr Samuel Wesley.

In 1731, many reports, concerning Mr John Wesley and his party, having reached his brother at Westminster, a correspondence took place between them on the subject; and in a letter written about this time, is a defence and explanation of their conduct. In one expression, concerning his hair, there is an apparent obscurity. But this may be obviated, by observing, that Mrs Wesley wished him to cut off his hair, which he took particular care of, and wore remarkably long: and an acquaintance of his at Oxford says, that he was remarked in the university for appearing with it smartly dressed and powdered, which at that time was rather uncommon. He has taken notice of this in another letter. " My mother's reason for my cutting off my hair is, be-,

caufe fhe fancies it prejudices my health.
As to my looks, it might doubtlefs mend
my complexion to have it off, by letting
me get a little more colour; and perhaps it might contribute to my making
a more genteel appearance. But thefe,
till ill health is added to them, I can't
perfuade myfelf to be fufficient grounds
for lofing two or three pounds a year. I
am ill enough able to fpare them."

This is undoubtedly a trifling fubject;
but it was neceffary to mention it, by way
of explaining what occurs in the following letter; as it will alfo ferve to fhow
how confcientious Mr Wefley was in the
fmalleft circumftances. The letter to
which we allude, is dated from Lincoln
college, November 17. 1731, and is ad
dreffed to his brother Samuel.

DEAR BROTHER,

Confidering the changes that I remember in myfelf, I fhall not at all wonder, if the time comes, when we differ
as little in our conclufions, as we now
do in our premifes. In moft we agree
already, efpecially as to rifing, not keeping much company, and fitting by a fire;
which I always do, if any in the room
does, whether at home or abroad. But
thefe are the things about which others
will never agree with me. Had I given
up thefe, or but one of them, rifing early (though I never am fleepy now) and
keeping little company; not one man in
ten, of thofe that are offended with me,
as it is, would ever open his mouth
againft any of the other particulars. For
the fake of thefe, thofe are mentioned.
The root of the matter lies here: would

I but employ a third of my money, and
half of my time as others do, smaller matters would be overlooked. But I think,
" nil tanti eſt." As to my hair, I am
much more ſure, that what this enables
me to do, is according to the Scripture,
than I am, that the length of it is contrary to it.

I have often thought of a ſaying of Dr
Haywood's, when he examined me for
prieſt's orders : " Do you know what
you are about? You are bidding defi-
ance to all mankind. He that would live
a Chriſtian prieſt, ought, whether his
hand be againſt every man or no, to expect that every man's hand ſhould be
againſt him." It is not ſtrange, that
every man, who is not a Chriſtian, ſhould
be againſt him that endeavours to be ſo;
but is it not hard, that even thoſe that
are with us ſhould be ſo? that a man's

enemies, in fome degree, fhould be thofe
of the fame houfehold of faith? Yet fo
it is: from the time that a man fets himfelf to this bufinefs, very many even of
thofe that travel the fame ground, many
of thofe who are before, as well as thofe
behind him, will lay ftumbling blocks in
his way. One blames him for not going.
faft enough; another for having made
no greater progrefs; another for going
too far; which, ftrange as it is, is the
more common charge of the two. For
this comes from people of all forts; not
only infidels, not only half Chriftians, but
fome of the beft men are apt to make
this reflection; " he lays unneceffary
burthens upon himfelf; he is too precife;
he does what God has no where required to be done." True: he has no
where required it of thofe who are
perfect; and even of thofe who are not,

all men are not required to ufe all means;
but every man is required to ufe thofe,
which he finds moft ufeful to himfelf.
And who can tell better than himfelf,
whether he finds them fo or no ? Who
knows the things of a man better than
the fpirit of a man, that is in him?

This being a point of no common concern, I defire to explain myfelf upon it,
once for all, and to tell you freely and
clearly thofe general pofitions, on which
I think I ground all thofe practices, for
which, as you would have feen, had you
read that paper through, I am generally
accufed of fingularity.

1ft, As to the end of my being, I lay
it down for a rule, that I cannot be too
happy, or therefore, too holy; and thence
I infer, that the more fteadily I keep my
eye upon the prize of my high calling,
the better; and the more of my thoughts,

and words, and actions are directly point
ed at the attainment of it.

2dly, As to the inftituted means of
attaining it, I likewife lay it down for a
rule, that I am to ufe them every time
that I may.

3dly, As to the prudential means, I
believe the rule holds, of things indifferent in themfelves; whatever I know to
do me hurt, that to me is not indifferont,
but refolutely to be abftained from: whatever I know to do me good, that to me
is not indifferent, but refolutely to be em-
braced.

But it will be faid, I am whimfical.
True; and what then? If by whimfical
be meant fimply, fingular, I own it: if
fingular without any reafon, I deny it
with both my hands, and am ready to
give a reafon to any who afks me, of
every cuftom wherein I differ from the

world. I grant, in many fingle actions,
I differ unreafonably from others; but
not wilfully; no: I fhall extremely thank
any one who will teach me to help it.
But can I totally help it, till I have more
breeding or prudence? To neither of
which I am naturally difpofed; and I
greatly fear, my acquired ftock of either
will give me fmall affiftance.

I have now but one thing to add, and
that is as to my being formal. If by this be
meant, that I am not eafy and unaffected
enough in my carriage, 'tis very true; but
how can I help it? I cannot be genteely
behaved by inftinct; and if I am to try after it by experience and obfervation of
others, that is not the work of a month,
but of years. If by formal be meant,
that I am ferious; this too, is very true:
but why fhould I help it? Mirth, I grant

is fit for you : but does it follow that it is fit for me ? Are the fame tempers, any more than the fame words and actions fit for all circumſtances ? If you are to " rejoice ever more," becauſe you have put your enemies to flight, am̄ I to do the fame, while they continually aſſault me ? You are glad, becauſe you are paſſed from death unto life ; well : but let him be afraid, who knows not whether he is to live or die.

Whether this be my condition or no, who can tell better than myſelf ? Him that can, whoever he be, I allow to be a proper judge, whether I do well to be generally as ſerious as I am.

J. W.

This letter needs no comment. It ſpeaks for itſelf, and is a lively portrait

of an ardent and fufceptible mind, in-
tently fixed upon it's object, and devoted
to the purfuit of thofe things, which to
him appeared of the utmoft importance.
We are far from prefuming, that Mr
Wefley made no miftakes, or that he fell
into no improprieties of fentiment or of
conduct. But from this and all the other
letters we have feen, it is evident that,
from the firft beginnings of Methodifm,
he was a man of fingular integrity; and
that the early imputations of fineffe and
felfifhnefs were falfe and unfounded ca-
lumnies.

Some time after Mr Wefley's ordination, he affifted his father at Epworth,
though we fuppofe he could only do it
occafionally, as he feems to have refided
chiefly at the univerfity. The old gentleman, finding himfelf upon the decline,

and anxious that the livir g fhould remain
in the family, wrote to his fon, intreat-
ing him to make intereft for the next
prefentation. The wifhes of the people,
the intereft of the family, and we may
add, it's very exiftence feemed to depend
upon his acquiefcence in this propofal.
But it could not be brought about. He
had conceived an invincible attachment
to Oxford, and had formed, from his
friends and advantages there, fuch ex-
pectations of religious improvement, as
rendered him unalterably determined
not to comply with their requeft.

This refufal was followed by feveral
letters from the parties concerned. We
fubjoin an extract of the firft of thefe,
which is from Mr Wefley's father, dated
November 20. 1734.

" Your ftate of the queftion, and only
argument is this; ' not whether I could

do more good to others, there or here ;
but whether I could do more good to
myfelf : feeing wherever I can be moft
holy myfelf, there I can moft promote holinefs in others.   But I can improve myfelf more at Oxford than at any other
place.'

"To this I anfwer, firft, it is not dear
felf, but the glory of God, and the different degrees of promoting it, which
fhould be our main confideration and
direction in the choice of any courfe of
life. Witnefs St. Paul and Mofes.—
2. Suppofe you could be more holy yourfelf at Oxford, how does it follow, that
you could promote holinefs more in others
there than elfewhere ? Have you found
many inftances of it, after fo many years
hard pains and labour ? Further : I dare
fay, you are more modeft and juft, than
to think there are no holier men than

you at Oxford : and yet it is possible
they may not have promoted holiness
more than you have done ; as I doubt
not, but you might have done it much
more, had you taken the right method;
for there is a particular turn of mind for
these matters ; great prudence as well
as fervour.

3. I cannot allow austerity or fasting,
considered in themselves, to be proper
acts of holiness ; nor am I for a solitary
life. God made us for a social life. We
must not bury our talent. We are to
let our light shine before men; and that,
not barely through the chinks of a bush-
el, for fear the wind should blow it out.
The design of lighting it was, that it
might give light to all that went into the
house of God : and to this academical
studies are only preparatory.

4. You are fenfible what figures thofe
make, who ftay in the univerfity till they
are fuperannuated. I cannot think drow-
finefs promotes holinefs. How com-
monly do they drone away their life,
either in a college or a country parfonage, where they can only give God the
fnuffs of them; having nothing of life
or vigour left, to make them ufeful in
the world.

5. We are not to fix our eye on one
fingle point of duty; but to take in the
complicated view of all the circumftances in every ftate of life that offers.
Thus, in the cafe before us, put all the
circumftances together. If you are not
indifferent whether the labours of an
aged father for above forty years, in
God's vineyard, be loft, and the fence
of it trodden down and deftroyed; if
you confider that Mr M—— muft in all

probability fucceed me, if you do not;
and that the profpect of that mighty Nim-
rod's coming hither, fhocks my foul,
and is in a fair way of bringing down my
grey hairs with forrow to the grave; if
you have any care for our family, which
muft be difmally fhattered, as foon as I
am dropt; if you reflect on the dear love
and longing of this poor people for you,
whereby you will be enabled to do God
fhe more fervice, and the plenteoufnefs
of the harveft, confifting of near two
thoufand fouls, whereas you have not
many more fcholars in the univerfity,
you may perhaps alter your will, and
bend your mind to him, who has pro-
mifed, " if in all our ways we acknowledge him, he will direct our paths."

This pathetic letter was followed by
another from his fon Samuel. His bro-

ther's chief objection was, as we have
feen already, that he could not leave
Oxford, upon the principle of doing
good, becaufe he was convinced, that
where he could reap the moft benefit
himfelf, he could more effectually promote the good of others. But, fays he,
" I am equally affured there is no place
under heaven, fo fit for my improvement
as Oxford."

A paffage in Samuel's letter, where
he contrafts his own obedience to his
father's injunctions, with the inflexible
behaviour of his brother, gives a ftriking
view of the opinion he had of his refolute and determined fpirit. The expreffions are very remarkable. " After this
declaration, I believe no one can move
your mind, but him that made it: much
lefs do I think myfelf qualified for that
purpofe.

" You may fay, I have been too paffive.
I left Oxford, with all the opportunity
of doing good, on a worldly account, at
my father's defire. I left my laft fettle-
ment, by the fame determination; and
I fhould have thought I finned both
times, if I had not followed it.

" You are not at liberty to refolve
againft undertaking a cure of fouls. You
are folemnly engaged to do it, before
God, and his high prieft, and his church.
Are you not ordained? Did you not
deliberately and openly promife to inftruct, to admonifh, to exhort thofe committed to your charge? Did you equi-
vocate then, with fo vile a refervation,
as to propofe in your heart, that you
would never have any fo committed?
'Tis not an univerfity; 'tis not a college;
'tis the order of the church according to
which you were called. Let Charles, if

he is filly enough, vow never to leave Oxford, and therefore avoid orders. Your
faith is already plighted to the contrary.
You have put your hand to the plough;
to that plough !

" I mention no lefs confiderations,
but reftrain myfelf; though not a little
furprifed, that you feem to hint what
never before entered the head of a Chriftian, that a parifh prieft cannot attain to
the higheft poffible perfection on this
fide heaven."

Mr Wefley s reply to thefe letters is
addreffed to his father, and contains fo
extenfive a view of the fubject, and fo
clear a detail of fome of the moft fingular of his opinions, that it is with regret
we omit it's infertion. But as it would
take up too much room in thefe memoirs,
we muft endeavour to extract the fub-
ftance of the arguments; referring the

reader, who may wifh for more accurate information, to the third Journal, page 29 to 37 of the fifth edition, printed in 1775. It is however to be obferved, that the letter publifhed in that Journal, is only an abridgement of the original, and fuch an abridgement as has confiderably defaced it, by the omiffion of fome of it's moft nervous and pointed expreffions.

After allowing, in the beginning of the letter his father's pofition, " that the glory of God, and the different ways of promoting it, are to be our fole confideration and direction in the choice of any courfe of life," he obferves " that courfe of life tends moft to the glory of God, in which we can moft promote holinefs in ourfelves and others;" and lays it down as incontrovertible, that " whatever ftate is beft for an individual, muft

be best for those who are to be instructed by him."

He then goes on to show, that Oxford
must be best for him, and conduce most
to his improvement, because there he
enjoyed the conversation of his select
friends, retirement, freedom from care
and from unprofitable company, beside
the advantages of public prayers twice
a day, and weekly communion. Speak-
ing of retirement, he introduces a reflection, which, were it not evident that he
is perfectly serious, might be considered
as a stroke of humour. " I have not only
as much, but as little company as I please.
I have no such thing as a trifling visit-
ant, except about an hour in a month,
when I invite SOME OF THE FELLOWS to
breakfast. Unless at that one time, no
one ever takes it into his head to set foot
within my door, except he has some bu-

finefs of importance to communicate to me, or I to him. And then, as foon as he has difpatched his bufinefs, he immediately takes his leave."

Without his prefent advantages, he contends, that it would not be poffible for him to guard 'for one month' againft intemperance in eating, drinking, and fleeping; againft irregularity in ftudy; againft lukewarmnefs in his affections and remiffnefs in his actions; and againft foftnefs and felf-indulgence, which he infifts, is "directly oppofite to that difcipline and hardfhip which become a foldier of Jefus Chrift." From thefe confiderations he fuppofes, that was he otherwife circumftanced, he muft become "an eafy prey to any impertinent company, to the cares of the world and the defire of other things, which would then roll back upon him with a full tide:" and he therefore concludes, that his refidence at Oxford was of abfolute neceffity and importance, and with him, related not merely to " the degrees of perfection, but to the very effence and exiftence" of his religious character ;

Agitur de vitâ et fanguine Turni.

" The point is, whether I fhall, or fhall not work out my falvation ; whether I fhall ferve Chrift or Belial."

From thefe obfervations, with regard to himfelf, he proceeds to an acknowledgment, that " God has made us for a focial life, to which academical ftudies are only preparatory;" and adds, that "there is not fo contemptible an animal upon earth, as one that drones away life, without ever labouring to promote the glory of God and the good of man ; that a fuperlative degree of contempt is, on all accounts, due to a college drone ; a

wretch that hath received ten talents,
and employs none; that is not only pro-
mifed a reward by his gracious Mafter,
but is paid before hand for his work
by his generous founder, and yet works
not at all; and that it is impoffible to fay
enough againft the drowfy ingratitude,
the lazy perjury of thofe, who are called
harmlefs or good fort of men, a fair proportion of whom I muft to our fhame
confefs, are to be fqund in colleges."

He does not however conclude his
philippic without putting in an exception.
" This will not conclude againft a college life in general. For the abufe does
not deftroy the ufe. Though there are
fome here, who are the lumber of the
creation, it does not follow, that others
may not be of more fervice to the world
in this ftation, than they could in any
other." Among other inftances, he fup-

pofes it may be fo with himfelf; for, fays
he, " I can be holier here than any
where elfe, if I faithfully ufe the bleffings
I enjoy. And to prove, that the holier
any man is himfelf, the more he will promote holinefs in others, there needs no
more than this one poftulatum; " the
help which is done upon earth, God doth
it himfelf." If fo; if God be the fole
agent in healing fouls, and man only the
inftrument in his hand, there can no
doubt be made, that the more holy a
man is, he will make ufe of him the
more, becaufe he is more willing to be
ufed; becaufe, the more pure he is, he
is the fitter inftrument for the God of
purity; becaufe he will pray more, and
more earneftly, that he may be employed, and that his fervice may tend to his
Mafter's glory; becaufe all his prayers,
for employment and fuccefs therein, will

more feverely pierce the clouds; becaufe, the more his heart is enlarged, the wider fphere he may act in without diftraction; and laftly, becaufe the more his heart is renewed in the image of God, the more God can renew it in others by him, without deftroying him by pride or vanity."

Among other arguments, for which he concluded, that he ought to remain at Oxford, he adds what he calls " the plenteoufnefs of the harveft;" or, in other words, the opportunity he had of doing good. " Here, fays he, are poor families to be relieved; children to be educated; work-houfes, in which both old and young want, and gladly receive the word of exhortation. Here are pri-fons to be vifited, wherein alone is a com-plication of all human wants : and laftly, here are the fchools of the prophets. Here are tender minds to be formed and strengthened; babes in Christ to be instructed and perfected in all useful learning. Of these in particular we must observe, that he who gains only one, does thereby as much service to the world as he could do in a parish in his whole life; for his name is legion; in him are contained all those who shall be converted by him. He is not a single drop of the dew of heaven, but a river, to make glad the city of God."

The argument employed by his father, when he tells him that Epworth was a " a large sphere of action, where he would have the charge of two thousand souls," he turns to his own purpose. " Two thousand souls! I see not how any man living can take care of one hundred; at least I could not; I know too well, ' quid valeant humeri.' Because the weight I

have already upon me is almoft more
than I am able to bear, ought I to increafe it tenfold?

——————————— " imponere Pelio Offam
Scilicet, atq. Offæ frondofum involvere Olympum."

To an objection, urged againft his refidence at Oxford, taken from the contempt and diflike, which he had acquired from his fingularities, he gives an
anfwer, that will furprife thofe who are
not well acquainted with his manner of
thinking on this fubject. He not only
denies that honour and reputation are
neceffary to ufefulnefs in the world, but
contends, that every " true Chriftian will
be contemned; that till he is fo, no man
is in a ftate of falvation; and that contempt is abfolutely neceffary to his doing
his full meafure of good in the world."
To eftablifh thefe pofitions, he adduces
the example of Chrift and his apoftles,

who were defpifed by wicked men; and
quotes thefe expreffions of our Lord,
" the fervant is not greater than his lord.
If they have perfecuted me, they will alfo
perfecute you. Becaufe ye are not of the
world, therefore the world hateth you."

He concludes the whole in the following language, as animated as any we remember to have feen from his pen.
" Where then is the fcribe? where is
the difputer of this world? where is the
replier againft God, with his fage maxims, he that is defpifed, can do no good
in the world. To be ufeful, a man muft
be efteemed. To advance the glory of
God, you muft have a fair reputation.'
Saith the world fo? But what faith the
Scripture? Why, that God hath laughed the heathen tongues of wifdom to
fcorn. It faith, that twelve defpifed followers of a defpifed mafter, all of whom

were of no reputation, who were efteemed as the filth and offfcouring of the
world, did more good in it, than all the
tribes of Ifrael. It faith, that the defpifed
Mafter of thefe defpifed followers left a
ftanding direction to us and our children, ' bleffed are ye,' not accurfed with
the heavy curfe of doing no good, of being ufelefs in the world, ' when men fhall
revile you and perfecute you, and fay all
manner of evil of you falfely, for my
name's fake. Rejoice and be exceeding
glad, for great is your reward in heaven.'

" Thefe are part of my reafons for
chufing to abide, till I am better informed, in the ftation wherein God has pla-
ced me. As for the flock committed to
your care, whom, for many years, you
have diligently fed ' with the fincere
milk of the word,' I truft in God your
labour fhall not be in vain, either to your-

(139)

felf or them. Many of them the Great
Shepherd has, by your hand delivered
from the hand of the deftroyer; fome
of whom are already entered into peace,
and fome remain unto this day For
yourfelf, I doubt not, but when your
‘ warfare is accomplifhed,’ when you are
‘ made perfect through fufferings,’ you
fhall come to your grave, not with forrow, but as a fhock of corn, full of years
and victories; and he that took care of
the poor fheep before you was born, will
not forget them when you are dead.”

The reply to this is by Samuel Wefley, junior, and dated Devon, February
8. 1734-5.

“ Your friends, retirement, frequent
ordinances, and freedom from care, are
great bleffings. All, except the laft, you
may expect in a lower degree elfewhere.
Sure all your labours are not come to

this, that more is abfolutely neceffary for you, for the very being of your Chriftian life, than for the falvation of all the parifh priefts in England! 'Tis very ftrange!

" To the queftion, ' what good have you done at Oxford,' you are not careful to anfwer; how comes it then, you are fo careful about the good you might do at Epworth ? ' The help that is done on earth, he doth it himfelf,' is a full folution of that terrible difficulty.

" The impoffibility of return, the certainty of being difliked by them that now cry you up, and the fmall comparative good my father has done, are good prudential reafons; but, I think, can hardly extend to confcience. You ' can leave Oxford when you will.' Not furely to fuch advantage. ' You have a probability of doing good there.' Will that

good be wholly undone, if you leave it?
Why should you not leaven another
lump?

" What you say of contempt is no
thing to the purpose; for, if you will go to
Epworth, I'll answer for it, you shall, in
a competent time, be despised as much
as your heart can wish. In your doctrine, you argue from a particular to a
general. To be useful, a man must be
esteemed, is as certain as any proposition
in Euclid; and I defy all mankind to
produce one instance of directly doing
spiritual good without it, in the whole
book of God.

" You join to contempt, hatred and
envy. But the first is very hardly con-
sistent, the latter utterly incompatible
with it; since none can envy another,
but for something he esteems.

" God, who provided for the flock

before, will do it after my father's death."
May he not fuffer them to be what they
once were, almoft heathens? And may
not this be prevented by your miniftry?

" It could never enter into my head,
that you could refufe on any other ground,
than a general refolution againft a cure
of fouls. I fhall give no pofitive reafon
for it, till my firft is anfwered. The order of the church ftakes you down; and
the more you ftruggle, will hold the faft-
er. If there be fuch a thing as truth, I
infift upon it, you muft, when opportunity offers, either perform that promife,
or repent of it: utrum mavis?"

This letter was anfwered as follows,
on the 15th of the fame month.

" Neither you nor I have any time to
fpare; fo I muft be as fhort as I can.

" There are two queftions between

us, one relating to being good; the other to doing good. With regard to the former, you allow I enjoy more of friends, retirement, freedom from care, and divine ordinances than I could elfewhere; and I add, 1. I feel this to be but juft enough. 2. I have always found lefs than this to be too little for me; and therefore, whatever others do, I could not throw up any part of it, without manifeft hazard to my falvation.

" As to the latter, I am not careful to anfwer what good I have done at Oxford, becaufe I cannot think of it, without the utmoft danger. I *am* careful about what good I may do at Epworth, firft, becaufe I can think of it without any danger at all; and fecondly, becaufe, as matters now ftand, I cannot avoid thinking of it without fin.

" Another can fupply my place at Epworth, better than at Oxford : and the
good done here is of a far more diffufive
nature. It is a more extenfive benefit, to
fweeten the fountain, than to do the fame
to particular ftreams.

" To the objection, ' you are defpifed
at Oxford, therefore you can do no good
there, I anfwer ; firft, a Chriftian will
be defpifed any where ; fecondly, no one
is a Chriftian, till he is defpifed; thirdly,
his being defpifed will not hinder his doing good, but much further it, by making him a better Chriftian. Without
contradicting any of thefe propofitions,
I allow, that every one, to whom you do
good directly, muft efteem you firft or
laft. N. B. A man may defpife you for
one thing ; hate you for a fecond ; and
envy you for a third.

" God may fuffer Epworth to be worfe
than before." But I may not prevent it
without hazard to my own foul.

" Your laft argument is ignoratio
elenchi, or implies thefe two propofi
tions ; firft, " you revolt againft any
parochial cure of fouls;" fecondly, " the
prieft who does not undertake the firft
parochial cure that offers, is perjured."
Let us add a third ; " the tutor who,
being in orders, never accepts a parifh,
is perjured :" and then I deny all three."

The following anfwer is without a date,
but we may fuppofe it was returned immediately.

" You fay, 'you have but juft enough.'
Had ever man on earth more? ' You
have experienced lefs to be infufficient.'
Not in the courfe of the priefthood, to
which you are called. In that way I am

perfuaded, though ' he that gathereth
much hath nothing over ; yet he that
gathereth little, hath no lacк '

' There is danger in thinking of the
good you have done ; but not of what
you may.' Vain glory lies both ways.
But the latter was your duty ; fo was
the former ; unlefs you can compare two
things, without thinking of one of them.

' The good at Oxford is more diffufive.' 'Tis not that good you have pro-
mifed. You deceive yourfelf, if you imagine you do not think of what you have
done. ' Your want may be better fup-
plied at Epworth.' Not if my father is
right in his fucceffions.

' A Chriftian will be defpifed every
where. No one is a Chriftian till he is
fo. It will further his doing good.' If
univerfal propofitions, I deny them all.
Efteem goes before the good done, as

well as follows after it. ' A man may
both defpife and envy. 'True. He may
have both a hot and cold fit of ague.
Contempt in general is no more compatible with, than neceffary to benefiting
others.

" I faid plainly, I thought you had
made a general refolution. As to taking
the firft offer, I fuppofed an opportunity,
a proper one; and now declare my judgment, fhould you live ever fo long, in
the ordinary courfe of providence, you
can never meet another fo proper.

' An ordained tutor, who accepts not
a cure is perjured.' Alter the term into,
' who refolves not to accept,' and I'll
maintain it, unlefs you can prove either
of thefe two ; firft, ' there is no obligation at taking orders ;'' fecondly, ' this
obligation is difpenfed with :' both which
I utterly deny."

Such was the controverfy on this important occafion. We do not fcruple to call it important; for fuch it certainly was; and fuch muft be every queftion, on the refult of which fhall depend the choice of that fituation, which is to give it's colour to every future circumftance of life.

In one refpect, the difputants feem to have been well fuited to each other. There was on both fides the ftricteft probity, and the moft unequivocal integrity. and it is obvious, that the conduct of Mr John Wefley was perfectly difinterefted. At leaft it was decidedly free from any bias on the fide of worldly intereft. The rectory of Epworth muft have been a fituation full as refpectable as a fellowfhip at Lincoln; and in all probability, confidering the ftrict difcipline of Mr Wefley, and the comparatively fmall

number of pupils he had under his tui-
tion, more advantageous. Of the labour
in either cafe, we fhall fay nothing. Whatever had been his fituation, it would have
made no difference with him. Such was
the activity of his mind, and fuch his
views of the neceffity of laborious ufefulnefs, that, whether he had accepted of
a living, or retained his fellowfhip, he
would equally have appeared, as he was
for more than fixty years, the moft dili-
gent and induftrious of mankind.

This conceffion, which the fulleft con-
viction of his integrity has extorted, lays
us under no neceffity of entirely appro-
ving his conduct, or of adjudging him
the victory in this debate. The judgment of moft of our readers, will give
the right fide of the argument to the
elder Mr Wefleys: and there are feveral reafons to incline us to the fame opi-

nion. The injunctions of a venerable,
declining parent, the welfare of a numerous and dependent family, and the un-
animous concurrence of a whole parish,
are confiderations of fuch moment, as to
leave us no difficulty in fuppofing, that
their voice was the voice of God. And
on a review of his objections, we cannot
help thinking, that feveral of thefe were
frivolous, and imaginary; that his religion had in it too much buftle and bufinefs, with too deep a tincture of aufte-
rity; that, in fome inftances, he impofed,
both on himfelf and others, a yoke not
impofed in the Scriptures, and which human nature is little calculated to fupport;
and that he conceived many things to be
neceffary, which we greatly doubt whether they were fo, even in his cafe; but
are certainly not neceffary to mankind
in general.

One exception we muſt make in his favour. Tho' we think it not in human nature to deſpiſe a good man, we are per-
ſuaded that there is, in all countries, a deſcription of men, ſo naturally and ſo uni-
verſally wicked and corrupt, as to have
conceived an invincible averſion to every
thing that is good. Perhaps we may go a
ſtep farther. They hate it as much, becauſe it is good, as becauſe it is contrary
to their own character and purſuits : and
like the Athenian, who was out of all patience with hearing ſo much of Ariſtides
the Juſt, they are ever ready to ſhow their
malignity againſt ſuperior merit. But
we hope, for the credit of humanity, that
this is not deſcriptive of a general character.

With this exception, we take the liberty of entering our caveat againſt one material part of Mr Weſley's argument.

K 4

His reasonings on the suppofition, that
contempt is neceffary to fuccefs in the
miniftry, though ably and ingenioufly
fupported, will fcarcely be affented to.
It appears indeed fo contrary to nature
and feeling, and is fo evidently oppofed
by reafon and obfervation, that we know
not how to admit it. From the hiftory
of our Saviour and the Apoftles, it does
not appear that their chief ufefulnefs was
in thofe places where they were defpifed
and oppofed, but on the contrary, where
they were moft efteemed and careffed.
The contempt which St. Paul found
among the Jews, was the reafon of his
departure to the Gentiles : and we find
it particularly noticed of one city, that
our Lord could not do " many mighty
works there, becaufe of their unbelief."
What is there underftood by unbelief is

obvious. They rejected his miſſion, and treated him with contempt.

Another circumſtance to be obſerved is, that Mr Weſley, as his brother takes notice, argues from a particular to a general. Becauſe the Jews, in the infancy of Chriſtianity, hated Jeſus Chriſt and his Apoſtles; and becauſe he had predicted, that they ſhould be expoſed in the courſe of their miniſtry to much perſecution, he thence infers that, in the more advanced ſtages of Chriſtianity, the ſame prejudices ſhould remain, and every Chriſtian be hated and deſpiſed by the majority of mankind. But it is by no means clear to us, that this reaſoning will ſtand the teſt. It has been contradicted, in thouſands of inſtances, by matter of fact. Many have there been in all ages of the moſt excellent characters, who not only did not ſuffer averſion and contempt,

(154)

but were univerfally beloved and efteemed. We give Addifon as an example.

The cafe of the Apoftles was peculiar.
The downfal of fuperftitions almoft co-
eval with the world, the deftruction of
polytheifm, and the extirpation of a religion, which the laxity, as well as abfur-
dity of it's principles, and the impurities
which it not only tolerated, but enjoined,
had rendered peculiarly pleafing to the
depraved and vicious tafte of it's votaries,
were the avowed objects of their miffion:
fo that the oppofition they had to con-
tend with, might naturally be expected.
We admit particular exceptions. There
may be exempt cafes and peculiar occafions, when good men are not treated as
they deferve. But in the prefent ftate of
the world, we need not fcruple to fay, that
where fuch perfons meet with decided and
general oppofition, the fault muft in a great

meafure originate with themfelves. There is a want of prudence or abilities, or fome defeſt in their judgment or deportment, which has a tendency to create diſlike, and to fruſtrate their good intentions. We fay this with the more confidence, as we fpeak from obfervation; having often heard fentiments from the pulpit, difguſtingly abfurd and indefenfible ; and having been witneſſes to improprieties and extravagancies in religious charaſters, which, though they did not amount to immorality, could not fail of the effeſt we have juſt mentioned.

It may be remarked, by the way, that there has been of late much falfe reafoning on thefe fubjeſts, from an idea, that there muſt be an exaſt parallel between Chriſtians of the prefent and apoſtolic age, and between the miniſters of every fubfequent period, and the apoſtles them-

felves. An idea, than which nothing
can be more abfurd. We might as well
fay, that every Chriftian minifter muft
be as capable as they were of healing the
fick or of raifing the dead! That we
ought to be as pious as the primitive
Chriftians, and the prefent minifters of
religion as anxious for the falvation of
mankind as the apoftles were, is indifpu-
tably true : but we deny, that fimilar
piety muft be neceffarily productive of
fimilar perfecution. To fuppofe this,
were to fuppofe, that to this moment,
Chriftianity has done nothing for mankind ; that the increafe of religion does
not check the fpirit of intolerance and
perfecution ; and that the world is, in
this age, as corrupt and flagitious, as il-
liberal and uninformed as in the earlieft
ages. All which is abfolutely falfe. Religious reformation, and the progrefs of

learning and fcience have long been in a certain degree proportioned to each other. The improvements in the arts of peace; the numerous inftitutions in almoft all countries, for humane and charitable purpofes; the more liberal manner in which war is conducted; with the comparatively fmall number who now fall a facrifice to the thirft of power and the ambition of princes, are full and unequivocal demonftrations of the mild and pacific influence of the religion of Jefus.

This is not all. The judgment of any candid and difpaffionate enquirer will at once decide upon thefe paradoxical pofitions; " to be ufeful, you muft be defpifed. The being contemned is abfolutely neceffary to a Chriftian's doing his full meafure of good in the world." How fo? Do men then go for inftruction to thofe they defpife? Are we difpofed to submit to the decisions of those, whose principles we abhor, and whose talents we hold in contempt? It is impossible. We must of necessity esteem a man who is useful to us; and the esteem must be prior to the usefulness. That "God will employ those most, who are fittest to be employed; that those are fittest, who are most holy; and that, as contempt is a glorious means of advancing holiness, God will most employ those who are most despised," is an argument that reminds us of the famous deduction of Themistocles, by which he proved, that his little boy governed the world. The failure of one link destroys the chain. Should it even be granted, that contempt may advance holiness, which will require some proof (for we have no great idea of "Beelzebub casting out Beelzebub") we are yet to re-

member, that a man may be fufficiently
in contempt, without the leaft capacity
for public ufefulnefs: and *that* contempt
is no fmall prefumption against him.
And though it fhould be granted, that
a bad man may hate his more excellent
neighbour for his piety and his excellencies, it is not in his power to defpife him.
Hatred and contempt are fcarcely con-
fiftent. Contempt and envy are totally
incompatible. Nor does it at all mend
the matter, to fay, that " a man may defpife you for one thing, hate you for a
fecond, and envy you for a third." We
are now confidering this defpifed perfon
in one fimple point of view, as a real
Chriftian: and in this view, it is not poffible that thefe contrary paffions fhould
be exercifed upon the fame object.

We have already hinted another objection, that ftruck us very forcibly;

and that is, that Mr Wesley was perhaps too positive, and depended too much on his own judgment. His father seems to have entertained the same idea, where he hints the necessity of " bending his mind to the will of God." When a man's own opinion is contrary to that of several of the most sensible people in the nation ; when these persons are his nearest relations ; and when their judgment so clearly concurs with the voice of a whole parish, it seems not improper to conclude, that there is in it something providential, and that he ought to doubt his own judgment, and to suspend his determinations.

And what friend of Mr Wesley's is there, so bigoted as to say, he could not be mistaken ? It is very possible, he might conceive some things to be materially hurtful, which were not so dangerous as he apprehended; and that he

might fuppofe his falvation abfolutely to
depend upon the fociety, and other advantages he enjoyed at Oxford, when in
reality it was not fo. Add to this, that
his reafonings on this fubject feem to argue too much confidence in outward
means, and too little in the grace of God:
as if it were impoffible he fhould be kept
from evil in the fame circumftances as
other men ; and as if (to ufe the language of his brother) ' more were neceffary to the very exiftence of his chriftian life, than to the falvation of every
other clergyman in the kingdom."
Strange indeed!

Thus, with the freedom of hiftory,
but without any intention of offence,
have we hazarded our opinion on this
occafion. And though we differ, and
prefume that moft people will differ from
Mr Wefley, and conceive that he faw

Vol. I.   L.

great difficulties, where in reality there
were none but what his own imagination
had created, it is impoffible not to ad-
mire and give him the full credit of his
confcientioufnefs and integrity. Perhaps
in this cafe his judgment was erroneous
and his reafonings inconclufive ; but it
muft at leaft be granted, that, as the
fubject prefented itfelf to his mind, he
could not, with a good confcience, have
acted otherwife than he did.

C H. A P. VI.

OF HIS MISSION TO AMERICA.

WHEN we firſt became acquainted with the ſubjeƈt of this chapter, it was not without ſome ſurprife.
Having ſeen in how determined a manner Mr Weſley had oppoſed himſelf to
the ſolicitations of his friends, with regard to Epworth, we naturally expeƈted,
that nothing leſs than ſtern neceſſity
could have induced him to quit his beloved retirement. The contrary however was the faƈt. In one of his excurſions to London, he met with a gentleman (Dr Burton) who was one of the
truſtees for the new colony at Georgia:

and was induced, by his folicitations, though with fome reluctance, to give up his pupils, and to leave his native country.

Not long after the correfpondence we have fo particularly confidered, we find him embarked. On the 14th of October 1735, accompanied by a Mr Ingham of Queen's College, Mr Delamotte, fon of a merchant in London, and his brother Charles, he went on board the Simmonds, off Gravefend, bound for Georgia. In the fame fhip was Mr Oglethorpe, who was afterwards a general officer, and died a few years ago at a very advanced age. Mr Wefley's chief object was the miffion to the Indians, whom, however, from the troubles that prevailed on the continent, he had little opportunity of inftructing.

While the fhip remained in the river,

(165)

he wrote to his brother Samuel, informing him, that he had prefented his father's Comment on Job to the Queen,
who rewarded him with many fmiles and
good words. In this letter he greatly
objects to the ufual mode of education;
finds fault with many of the claffics, efpecially Ovid, Virgil, and Terence's Eu-
nuch, as being calculated to inflame the
fenfual appetites, and to cherifh the love
of grandeur and ambition; and as totally
contrary to that purity of heart, which,
he obferves, is much more important than
elegance of ftyle. He tells him, that he,
as well as himfelf, was called to the converfion of heathens; that his fcholars
were fo many fouls committed to his care,
to prepare them for eternity; and that he
therefore conjured him to banifh the claffics, with their poifon, from his fchool, and
introduce, inftead of them, fuch chrifti-

an authors as would work, together with him, in " building up his flock in the knowledge and love of God."

Here again we are conftrained to enter our diffent; having no idea that the languages can be taught with any propriety, or to any degree of perfection, but by the claffics. But in this inftance, his opinion in 1735 and in 1777 was exactly contradictory. In the fecond volume of the Arminian Magazine, is a letter from a clergyman, who afks whether a religious fchoolmafter may ufe the claffics in his fchool ; and he anfwers, " doubtlefs he may." We cite this as one proof, among others, that, in the latter part of life, he was lefs rigid than in his youth.

On Friday, the 17th of October, the fhip being ftill in the river, he preached without notes, and adminiftered the facrament on the quarter deck. The firft

time of his preaching in this manner was
accidental. He had gone to Allhallows',
in London, to hear Dr Heylin, who, at
that time, was much followed. The Doctor not coming, Mr Wefley was requeft-
ed to fupply his place; and having no
notes about him, he preached extem-
pore.

By heavy gales and contrary winds,
he was detained fome time in the
channel, and did not get out to fea till
the 10th of December. Among the
paffengers were twenty-fix Germans,
who were going to fettle in America:
and here commenced his acquaintance
with the Moravian brethren, which he
cultivated for fome time with great affiduity. He gives them an excellent character, and particularly commends their
humble and chriftian deportment during
the paffage, and their calm and refolute

behaviour in the moment of danger.

Nitchman, the Moravian bifhop, began to learn Englifh, Mr Wefley German, and Mr Delamotte Greek. Mr Charles Wefley wrote fermons, and Mr Ingham inftructed the children. To fhew Mr Wefley's love of difcipline, and and his fondnefs for doing every thing by rule, it will not be amifs to tranfcribe his account of the manner in which they fpent the day. " We now began to be a little regular. From four in the morning till five, each of us ufed private prayer. From five to feven we read the Bible together, carefully comparing it (that we might not lean to our own underftandings) with the writings of the earlieft ages. At feven we breakfafted ; at eight were the public prayers. From nine to twelve, learnt the languages, and inftructed the children. At twelve we

met, to give an account to one another
what we had done fince our laft meeting, and what we defigned to do before
our next. At one we dined. The time
from dinner to four we fpent in reading
to thofe, of whom each of us had taken charge, or in fpeaking to them feve-
rally, as need required. At four were
the evening prayers; when either the
fecond leffon was explained (as it always
was in the morning) or the children were
catechifed and inftructed before the congregation. From five to fix we again
ufed private prayer. From fix to feven
I read in our cabin to two or three of
the paffengers, of whom there were about
eighty Englifh on board, and each of my
brethren to a few more in theirs. At
feven I joined with the Germans in their
public fervice; while Mr Ingham was
reading between the decks, to as many as

defired to hear. At eight we met again, to inftruct and exhort one another. Between nine and ten we went to bed, where neither the roaring of the fea, nor the motion of the fhip, could take away the refrefhing fleep which God gave us."

None can fay that the time was not well filled up. But we doubt whether fo unremiting an attention and fuch a multiplicity of bufinefs is not too much for the human mind. We remember the obfervation " neque femper arcum tendit Apollo." If the bow be not fometimes unftrung, it will foon lofe it's elafticity. We fufpect too, that rough weather, and the various changes incident to a paffage by fea, muft frequently have interrupted this œconomy.

On Thurfday, the 15th of January, 1736, feveral were much exafperated

with Mr Wefley, for having complained
to Mr Oglethorpe of the unequal diftri-
bution of water, which was put into better hands. From the 17th to the 25th
they had violent ftorms; the fea going
frequently over the fhip, and breaking
through the cabin windows. He obferves that the " Englifh were exceedingly frightened, while the Germans,
men, women, and children were perfectly calm," which he afcribes to the power of religion. From the Germans, fays
he, " I went to their trembling neighbours, and pointed out the difference in
the hour of trial, between him that ferveth God, and him that ferveth him
not."

On the 29th they fell in with the fkirts
of a hurricane, which however did no
damage; on the 4th of February they
faw land; and on the 6th, after a ftor-

my paffage, firft fet foot on fhore, on a
fmall uninhabited ifland, near Tybee,
where they kneeled down and returned
God thanks. Mr Oglethorpe immediately fet off for Savannah.

During this paffage it was that Mr
Wefley, "judging it might be helpful"
to him, difcontinued the ufe of flefh and
wine, and confined himfelf to vegetables,
chiefly rice and bifket. He alfo left off
eating fuppers ; and his bed having been
wet by the fea, he lay upon the floor,
and flept found till morning. He adds,
"I believe, I fhall not find it needful to
go to bed, as it is called, any more."

While the fhip lay off Tybee, feveral
Indians came on board, fhook hands,
and welcomed them to America. They
expreffed a defire to be inftructed, as
foon as they were at liberty from the
confufions of war ; but added, " we

would not be made chriftians as the Spaniards make chriftians; we would be taught before we are baptized. " It is fubmitted to the judicious reader, how far Mr Wefley's reply to thefe Indians was juft and feafonable. " There is but one, he that fitteth in heaven, who is able to teach man wifdom. Though we are come fo far, we know not whether he will pleafe to teach you by us or no. If he teaches you, you will learn wifdom; but we can do nothing." He defcribes them as being tall, well proportioned men, with a remarkable foftnefs in their fpeech, and gentlenefs in their whole behaviour. From the converfations he and other Europeans had with the Indians, it appears that their notions of religion were very crude and imperfect; that they had fome idea of the interpofition of invifible beings, in the govern-

ment of the world; and fome notion of
the morality or immorality of certain actions. They thought it foolifh in white
men to build great houfes, as if they were
to live for ever; and condemned that
practice, fo common among the favages,
of taking medicines to procure abortion.

At Savannah Mr Wefley became acquainted with Mr Spangenberg and.
other Germans, and attended at the con-
fecration of a bifhop; when he tells us,
that the fimplicity and folemnity of the occafion made him almoft forget the feven-
teen hundred years between, and imagine
himfelf in one of thofe affemblies, 'where
form and ftate were not; but Paul, the
tentmaker, or Peter, the fifherman, prefided; yet with the demonftration of the
fpirit and with power.'

By the direction of Mr Oglethorpe,
a houfe was built for the miffionaries,
who, on their arrival at Savannah, were
received with great cordiality. Mr Wefley entered upon his miniftry, on Sunday, the 7th of March 1736, by preaching from the epiftle for the day; and
obferves that, when he faw the number
of people crowding into the church, the
deep attention with which they received
the word, and their ferioufnefs afterwards, he " could not believe, that this
ferious, attentive people fhould afterwards trample under foot that word, and
fay all manner of evil falfely of him that
fpake it."

Colonifts have generally been remark
ed as an obftinate and ungovernable people; but perhaps the fault was not wholly in the Georgians. The Americans are
not to be managed, but by a delicate and

skilful hand. His father had obferved to him, that, in order to do good to mankind, " a particular talent is neceffary, great prudence as well as fervor." Mr Wefley's conduct (to fay the leaft of it) was, on many occafions, capricious and fanciful : in fome inftances, abfolute and defpotic. He gave great offence by infifting upon baptizing their children by immerfion, which, though provided for in the rubrick, was not at all neceffary, and which no clergyman did but himfelf; while his experiments upon his own conftitution, firft, leaving off meat and wine; then giving up fuppers, and laftly, confining himfelf to bread, in order to try " whether life might not be fuftained by one fort, as well as by variety of food," were by no means calculated to imprefs his parifhioners with the moft favourable opinion of his judgment. It is not pretended there could be any intrinfic evil in fuch experiments; but they certainly were not judicious. They had at leaft a whimfical afpect, and induced in many who obferved him, a fufpicion, that he laid too great a ftrefs on bodily aufterities and trifling circumftances, which have nothing to do with a man's falvation, nor any neceffary connection with his chriftian character. Mr Wefley was of the contrary opinion; as will appear from his own words, written when he firft entered upon his bread diet. "To the pure all things are pure. Every creature is good to them, and nothing to be rejected. But let them, who know and feel that they are not thus pure, ufe every help and remove every hindrance; always remembering, he that defpifeth little things, fhall fall by little and little."

Vol. I.   M

During his refidence on the continent, he frequently laboured, not only with his tongue, but with his hands ; and continued his cuftom of eating little, of fleeping lefs, and of leaving not a moment unemployed. In fome refpects he was admirably calculated for a miffionary in a cold, inhofpitable clime. For fo fmall a perfon, he poffeffed great mufcular ftrength, a found and vigorous conftitution, with a moft ardent and indefatigable mind. He expofed himfelf, with the utmoft indifference, to every change of feafon, and inclemency of weather. Snow and hail, ftorm and tempeft had no effect on his iron body. He frequently lay down on the ground, and flept all night, with his hair frozen to the earth. He would fwim over rivers, with his cloaths on, and travel till they were dry ; and all this without any apparent injury to his health. He feems alfo to have poffeffed great prefence of mind and intrepidity in danger. Going from Savannah to Frederica, the pettiawga, in which he was, came to an anchor. He wrapt himfelf up in a cloak, and went to fleep upon deck : but, in the courfe of the night, he rolled out of his cloak, and fell into the fea, fo faft afleep, that he did not perceive where he was, till his mouth was full of water. He fwam round to a boat, and got out.

On his arrival at Frederica, he found his brother exceeding weak, from the flux, with which he had been fome time confined : but he recovered from the moment he faw him! The medical men would fay, that the joy, occafioned by his arrival, had a fudden effect on his conftitution, and gave an impulfe to the fyftem, favourable to convalefcence. Mr

Wefley faw it in another point of view, and fays, " this hath God wrought !"

Returning to Savannah, they agreed to advife the people, thofe who were the moft ferious, to form themfelves into a fociety, and to meet once or twice a week, in order to reprove, inftruct, and exhort one another ; and, from thefe, to felect a fmaller number, for a more in-timate union. With each of thefe divi-fions the two brothers frequently con-verfed, and met them all together, on Sundays, at Mr Wefley's houfe. Here was the origin of the future œconomy of claffes and bands.

On Sunday, the 9th of May 1736, he began to divide the public prayers into three fervices, in conformity to the ori-ginal inftitution of the church. The morning fervice began at five ; the com-munion office and fermon at eleven ;

the evening fervice at three. Mr Oglethorpe, on his return from the fouth,
gave orders againft the profanation of
the Lord's day, by fifhing and fowling;
and Mr Wefley fummed up, at Frederica, what he had feen and heard among
them, inconfiftent with chriftianity.——
" Some were profited, and the reft deep-
ly offended."

From this time, the offence became
general. Many of his friends grew
fhy. They confidered his fermons as
fatires upon particular perfons; and fome
determined they would hear him no
more. He now obferves that, during a
violent thunder ftorm, he found he had
not yet conquered the fear of death.
Going for Charleftown with his brother,
who was about to embark for Europe,
they were in danger of overfetting in a
boat. The maft fell, through the vio-

M 3

lence of the ftorm, but the failors got it into the boat, and, by a vigorous exertion, rowed on fhore.

On his return to Savannah, finding Mr Oglethorpe was gone, he ftayed only one day; and leaving Mr Ingham and Mr Delamotte, fet out once more for Frederica. In walking to Thunderbolt, he was exceffively wet by the rain; and obferves, that the general idea of the unwholefomenefs of the rains and dews, in America, is a mere vulgar error; that he had frequently been wet with the rains, and had lain many nights expofed to the dew, without the leaft injury. And fo, continues he, " might any one, if his conftitution were not impaired by the foftnefs of a genteel education!"

If the parifhioners of Savannah and Frederica did not receive much benefit from his inftructions, it certainly was not

for want of diligence on his part. He
feems to have been fully employed, during his refidence among them, as will
appear from the account publifhed in his
hiftory of methodifm, which we infert in
his own words. " On the Lord's day,
the Englifh fervice lafted from five to
half paft fix. The Italian (with a few
Vaudois) began at nine. The fecond
fervice for the Englifh, including the fermon and the holy communion, continued from half paft ten till about half paft
twelve. The French fervice began at
one. At two I catechifed the children.
About three began the Englifh fervice.
After this was ended, I joined with as
many as my largeft room would hold,
in reading, prayer, and finging praife.
And about fix, the fervice of the Germans began, at which I was glad to be

M 4

prefent, not as a teacher, but as a
learner.''

What immenfe labour was this! And
what an idea muft it give us of his in-
duftry and perfeverance, if we confider,
that, befides the French and Italian,
which we know not whether he acquired
here or at Oxford, he learnt German,
that he might converfe with the Moravians, and Spanifh, for the fake of his
Jewifh parifhioners!

We particularly notice a remark he
makes about this time. He had been
fent for to a perfon, who became a convert from popery. On this occafion he
obferves, that he had received many ad-
vices to beware of the increafe of popery, but not one caution againft the progrefs of infidelity; which, fays he, is a
little extraordinary; for, '' in every place
where I have yet been, the number of

(185)

converts to popery bore no proportion
to that of the converts to infidelity."
He adds, that as bad a religion as popery is, no religion is ftill worfe; that the
ftate of a deift is more dangerous than
that of a papift; and that he had "known
many of the latter reconverted, but not
one of the former." There is undoubtedly much propriety in thefe remarks
It is certain however, that deifts have
fometimes been reconverted. Lord Rochefter is a memorable inftance: and,
if we miftake not, Mr Wefley himfelf
has had the pleafure, fince that time, of
feeing feveral examples of the fame kind.
But the good catholics will hardly thank
him for the affociation; though many of
our readers will perhaps join him in fuppofing, that to allow popery to be better
than infidelity, is to fay all that can be
faid upon it.

Of his ufefulnefs in America, as we
have little information, we can form no
accurate conception. All that we can
learn of it, muſt be from his own account, which is as follows: " All in
Georgia have heard the word of God.
Some have believed, and begun to run
well. A few ſteps have been taken to-
wards publiſhing the glad tidings, both
to the African and American Heathens.
Many children have learned how they
ought to ſerve God, and to be uſeful to
their neighbour. And thoſe, whom it
moſt concerns, have an opportunity of
knowing the true ſtate of their infant
colony, and laying a firmer foundation
of peace and happineſs to many genera-
tions." By the African heathens, we
ſuppoſe he means the ſlaves that were
brought to the continent; and by the
ſteps taken for the inſtruction of them

and the Indians, we are moſt likely to
underſtand, the ſchool, called Irene,
erected for them, under the inſpection
of Mr Ingham. Of the ſucceſs of it we
have not heard.

That his ſituation abroad was, upon
the whole, extremely unpleaſant, we have
no doubt. But the moſt unfortunate
event that befel him, was his difference
with Mr Cauſton, who was ſtorekeeper
and chief magiſtrate of Savannah. Not
long before this happened, he complained, in a letter to a friend, that he could
not conceive how he " could attain to
the being crucified with Chriſt," being in
a condition he neither deſired nor ex-
pected in America, in eaſe, honour, and
abundance. As for the eaſe and honour
of his ſituation, we know nothing of it:
but the abundance he complains of was
certainly no great matter ; for the ex-

pences of Mr Delamotte and himfelf, for
one whole year, did not amount to forty-
five pounds. The caufe of complaint,
fo far at leaft as it related to eafe and
honour, was prefently removed. The
calm was fucceeded by a ftorm. Meeting with Mr Spangenberg, on his way to
to Ebenezer, he mentioned his fituation;
and having confulted him, with regard
to the conduct he fhould purfue, determined to follow his advice.

Mr Wefley informs us, that he had
reproved Mrs Williamfon, Mr Caulton's
niece, for fomething in her behaviour,
that he difapproved. The reproof was
highly refented by the lady. Soon after
he repelled her from the communion;
in confequence of which, a warrant was
ferved upon him, and he was brought
before one of the bailiffs and the record-
er. Refufing to acknowledge their au-

thority, in a matter purely ecclefiaftical,
he was ordered to appear at the next
court held for Savannah. After fome
fharp words on the part of Mr Caufton,
Mr Wefley wrote to his niece, telling her,
that if fhe offered herfelf at the table,
on the next Sunday, he would inform
her, as he had done before, wherein fhe
had done wrong; and then, fays he,
" when you have openly declared yourfelf to have truly repented, I will admi-
nifter to you the myfteries of God."

This was judged rather an aggrava-
tion, than a reparation of the offence.
Mr Caufton then declared he would have
fatisfaction, and foon after told many perfons, that Mr Wefley " had repelled So-
phy from the communion, becaufe fhe
had rejected his propofals of marriage,
and married Mr Williamfon." On this
occafion he takes notice of the " graci-

ous providence of God, in the leſſons
for the week," which turned chiefly on
encouragements to patience under ſuf-
ferings. His chief fear ſeems to have
been, leſt this affair ſhould have induced
the people to abſent themſelves from the
ſervice: but his fears were diſappointed.
The congregation was more numerous
than uſual; and many, he informs us,
took notice of thoſe words, in the firſt
leſſon, "ſet Naboth on high among the
people, and ſet two men, ſons of Belial
before him, to bear witneſs againſt him."

It is ſaid that, when the time of trial
approached, a jury was packed by his
antagoniſt, compoſed of a papiſt, a
Frenchman, an infidel, and about twenty diſſenters and others, who, having perſonal quarrels with Mr Weſley, had openly vowed revenge. A charge was given
by Mr Cauſton, to beware of ſpiritual

tyranny, and to oppofe the illegal authority that was ufurped over their confci-
ences ; and a long lift of grievances was
found by the grand jury, though not
without a proteft from feveral of the
jurors. Mr Wefley moved for an immediate hearing, which, on various pre-
tences, was put off; when, having confulted feveral of his friends, and put up
advertifements of his intentions to return
to England, notwithftanding an order to
detain him, on the 2d of December 1737,
he " fhook off the duft of his feet, for a
teftimony againft them," and left Georgia, having preached the gofpel there (to
ufe his own words) not as he ought, but
as he was able, one year and nearly nine
months.

Such was the leave our miffionary
took of America, to which he never returned. This affair has been varioufly,

but we fufpeƈt, in no inftance accurate-
ly, related. The editors of the Gofpel
Magazine fay, that he left Savannah by
night, and on foot, to elude the terrors
of a court of juftice. We follow the
account, defeƈtive as it is, which he publifhed in the Journals. But, on a review
of the tranfaƈtion, we are particularly
ftruck with the oontraft between the
reception he met with, and the honour
and popularity of Mr Whitefield, in every
part of the continent. It is much to be
lamented by Mr Wefley's friends, that,
though his American enemies evidently
aƈted in a moft violent and unjuft manner, his reƈtitude of conduƈt is not fo
clear as might be wifhed. He does not
tell us of what nature was his complaint
againft Mrs Williamfon: nor does he
deny that he had made his addreffes to
this lady; which, if not true, he cer-

tainly ought to have contradicted in the moft exprefs terms; for, on this circum-ftance, the public opinion muft be ne-ceffarily fufpended. If it was true, his behaviour will be naturally afcribed to the phrenzy of difappointed love. If not, fome other reafon muft remain in referve. But on this queftion it is im-poffible to decide. We may conjecture; but we cannot fpeak with certainty.

His brother Charles finding the cli-mate to difagree with his conftitution, had failed for England in July 1736. Mr Ingham left Savannah on the 26th of January 1737. How long Mr Delamotte remained, we are not informed.

Mr Wefley does not bid adieu to the continent, without relating fome melan-choly inftances of the cruelty and vil-lanies of the mafters of fhips, while the rage for emigration was fo prevalent.

It is indifputable, that they ufed infinite art to induce farmers and tradefmen to embark for this land of promife; when, after borrowing their money, and plundering them of their property, they fold them to the planters. The confequence, in many inftances, one of which is related by Mr Wefley, was diftraction and fuicide.

He alfo gives an account of the fituation of Georgia, it's foil, produce, cultivation, and inhabitants. But we have fome doubt of the correctnefs of the portrait. The colouring partakes rather too much of the *fombre*; and we perceive, whenever he has occafion to fpeak of America, certain traits of prejudice, that we can eafily account for, but which are fcarcely worthy a philofopher and a citizen of the world.

He gives the following fhocking character of the Georgian Indians: " Every one does that which is right in his own eyes; and if it appears wrong to his neighbour, the perfon aggrieved, fteals on the other unawares, and fhoots him, fcalps him, or cuts of his ears: having only two fhort rules of proceeding, to do what he will, and what he can. They are all, except perhaps the Choctaws, gluttons, drunkards, thieves, diffemblers, liars. They are implacable, unmerciful murderers of fathers, murderers of mothers, murderers of their own children; it being a common thing for a fon to fhoot his father or mother, becaufe they are old and paft labour; and for a woman either to procure abortion, or to throw her child into the next river, becaufe fhe will go with her hufband to the war. Indeed hufbands, ftrictly fpeaking, they have none; for any man leaves

his wife, fo called, at pleafure; who frequently, in return, cuts the throats of all
the children fhe has had by him. Whore-
dom they account no crime, and few inftances appear of a young Indian woman's refufing any one. Nor have they
any fixed punifhment for adultery; only
if the hufband take his wife with another
man, he will do what he can to both,
unlefs fpeedily pacified by the prefent of
a gun or a blanket." That this horrid
picture has it's originals in real life, we
have no doubt, but we cannot admit
it as an univerfal likenefs. We know,
on the contrary, that there are many exceptions; and that Europeans have often
owed their lives to the clemency of
Indians.

Mr Wefley, difappointed in the prime
object of his miffion, embarked for Europe, at Charleftown, on Thurfday, the

22d of December, 1737, made the Lizard-point on the 29th of January, and after a pleafant paffage, landed at Deal, on the 1ft of February, 1738. Mr Whitefield failed through the channel for America, as he entered it, on his return. On the 3d he came to London, after an abfence of two years and four months.

N 3

CHAP. VII.

His Reflections on his Arrival; his Conversion and Journey to Hernhuth and Marienburn.

ABOUT this time he obferves, that his mind was full of thought; and that he wrote down part of what occurred to him, as follows : " It is now two years and almoft four months fince I left my native country, to teach the Georgian Indians the nature of chriftianity : but what I have learned myfelf in the mean time? Why, what I leaft of all fufpected, that I, who went to America, to convert others, was never myfelf converted to God. I am not mad, though I thus fpeak; but I fpeak the words of

truth and fobernefs; if haply fome of
thofe, who ftill dream, may awake, and
fee that as I am, fo are they." The re-
mainder of this foliloquy, remarkable as
it is, there is no need to tranfcribe.
What we are now concerned with, is
the tendency of it; and that is, to fhew
that, notwithftanding his zeal, his labours, his fincerity, his charity, and his
punctual obfervance of the means of
grace, he " was not a chriftian, becaufe
he had not faith." His notion of faith
is, " a fure truft and confidence that a
man hath, that, through the merits of
Chrift, his fins are forgiven, and he re-
conciled to the favour of God." So far
he agrees with the church of England.
How far his idea of the mode of communi-
cation will be deemed orthodox, is another queftion. He fuppofes, and we believe
it is the doctrine of the Moravian bre-

N 4

thren, from whom it was derived to the first methodifts, that this confidence is conveyed by an immediate influence of the Holy Spirit, who is fuppofed, by a ftrong perfuafion, in fome way or other, directly communicated to the mind, to reveal this important circumftance. This is called by fome divines, " the faith of affurance :" and it is one of thofe peculiar doctrines, in which Mr Wefley is fuppofed to differ from moft of the proteftant churches. As we fhall probably give this fubject a more particular confideration in the fequel, we difmifs it for the prefent.

But we cannot pafs over Mr Wefley's reflections on his own ftate, without remarking a difficulty we are under. Of his own character he muft be allowed to be the beft judge. But how fhall we reconcile him with himfelf? On his re-

turn from Georgia, in 1738, he fays he
was not a chriftian. The Journal in
which this is faid, was publifhed in 1775:
and yet, giving an account in this fame
Journal, of himfelf, and of what he judged to be his ftate in 1729, when he declared his perfuafion, that he was " even
then in a ftate of falvation," he adds, in
a note at the bottom, " and I believe I
was *." How thefe paffages can be made
to agree, we are at a lofs to difcover:
fince it is generally underftood among
the orthodox divines, that if a man has
not faith, he is not a chriftian; and if
not a chriftian, confequently, not in a
ftate of falvation. There is indeed a
diftinction of his, which, if there were
any thing in it, might poffibly do fomething toward reconciling this contradic-

* See 1ft Journal, page 68; and 2d Journal,
page 26. Edition 1775.

tion. He fays, in one place, that he
" *had the faith of a fervant, but not of a
fon*.*" But we doubt the propriety of
this diftinction. Does he mean here,
what is called in Scripture, a " fervant
of God," or does he not? If not, he
could have no true faith, and therefore
could not be in a ftate of falvation. But
if he does, then we fay, that in this refpect, the Scripture knows no difference
between the phrafes, " fons of God and
fervants of God;" confequently, here is
a diftinction without a difference.

During his refidence at London, where
he was detained feveral weeks by the
truftees for Georgia, he informed his
friends of fome reafons, which haftened
his return to England; and, being advifed
to relate them to the truftees, he waited

* See note, 2d Journal, page 17. Edition 1775.

twice on Mr Oglethorpe, without having
an opportunity to explain : but, attending foon after at the board, he gave them
an account of the colony, fo little flatter-
ing, and fo contrary to that which had
been given them by others, that he fuppofes fome of them never forgave him.

It was at this time that he preached in
many of the churches in town ; but fuch
was the effect of his unfafhionable doctrine, that after the firft fermon in every
church, he was generally informed, he
muft preach there no more. The doctrine, to which we particularly allude,
is what he calls " faving faith," which,
he informs us, he faw clearly on Monday
March the 6th, 1738, and " declared it
without delay." The confequence of
this mode of preaching, he fays, was,
that God then began to work by his miniftry, as he had never done before.

He now spent some time in visiting
some of his friends and relations; met
with Peter Böhler, Schulius Richter,
and other Moravians just landed from
Germany; in whose company and conversation he expresses a particular satis-
faction. Soon after, going to Oxford
to see his brother Charles, who was
said to be dying, he found him recover-
from the pleurisy. Here he again met
with Böhler, who thought him too phi-
losophical, or too rational (for we cannot tell which) and laconically told him,
" mi frater, mi frater, philosophia ista
tua excoquenda est." It was by him,
he tells us, he was convinced of the want
of that faith, whereby alone we are saved;
and by his advice he began to preach
" salvation by faith alone." Peter's words
are remarkable: " preach faith till you
have it; and then, because you have it,

you will preach faith." The firſt to
whom he preached this doſtrine, was a
priſoner under ſentence of death. The
effeſt is not mentioned.

Much of this ſpring was ſpent in tra-
velling with Mr Kinchin, a fellow of Cor-
pus, to Mancheſter, Holms Chapel, New-
caſtle in Staffordſhire, and ſeveral other
towns, where they frequently preached
and exhorted, either embracing or making occaſions of ſpeaking in public and
private, in inns and ſtables, and where-
ever they came, on matters of religion,
and with various ſucceſs. Some ſtared
in ſilent aſtoniſhment at their reproofs
and exhortations; while others ſeemed
thankful and willing to receive inſtruction. In ſome inſtances, prudence held
their tongues, and prevented them from
embracing opportunities of ſpeaking to
thoſe who attended them at their inns,

and in other places; and Mr Wefley mentions fome occafions, in which he fuppofes they were providentially rebuked for their negligence. Among others he gives the following inftance : " The next day, March. 11th, we dined at Birmingham, and foon after we left it, were reproved for our negligence there (in letting thofe, who attended us, go without either exhortation or inftruction) by a fevere fhower of hail!"

In the latter end of March, or the beginning of April, he left off his cuftom of confining himfelf to a form of prayer. This change firft took place at the Caftle in Oxford, where he and Mr Kinchin went to vifit a prifoner. They firft prayed in feveral forms, and then in " fuch words as were given them in that hour." The man kneeled down in " great heavinefs and confufion." After a fhort space he rose up, and eagerly said, "I am now ready to die. I know Chrift has taken away my fins, and there is no more condemnation for me." He adds, "the fame compofed chearfulnefs he fhewed, when carried to execution: and in his laft moments he was the fame, enjoying a perfeft peace, in confidence, that he was *accepted in the Beloved.*" Mr Wefley again obferves, that, "on Monday, April 1ft, being at Mr Fox's fociety, his heart was fo full, that he could not confine himfelf to the ufual forms; and that he did not propofe to be confined to them any more, but to pray indifferently, with a form or without, as he fhould find fuitable to particular occafions."

At this time, his mind having been warmed by the difcourfes of his Moravian friends, he was waiting in anxious

expectation for his own converfion. He
fays, that he had now no objection to
what Böhler had faid of the nature of
faith, and of the holinefs and happinefs,
which he defcribed as the fruit of it.
But he could not comprehend what he
fpoke of an inftantaneous work. He
could not underftand, "how this faith
fhould be given in a moment; how a
man could at once be thus turned from
darknefs to light, from fin and mifery,
to righteoufnefs and joy in the Holy
Ghoft." To fatisfy himfelf on this fubject, he fearched the Scriptures, particularly the Acts of the Apoftles; and
the refult was, that, to his utter aftonifh-
ment, he "found fcarce any other inftances there, than inftantaneous converfions; fcarce any fo flow as that of St.
Paul, who was three days in the pangs
of the new birth." The only retreat he

now had, was in the difference between the present and the primitive times. He was persuaded, that " God wrought thus in the first ages of christianity;" but the times being changed, he was not certain that he would " work in the same manner now."

On Sunday, the 22d of April, he was driven out of this retreat, by " the concurring testimony of several living witnesses, who declared, that God had thus wrought in themselves, giving them, in a moment, such a faith in the blood of his son, as translated them out of darkness into light, out of sin and fear into holiness and happiness." Here, says he, ended my disputing. I could only cry out, " Lord, help thou my unbelief."

His persuasion of the truth of this doctrine was increased, as he informs us, by " hearing the experiences of Mr Hut-

Vol. I.   O

chins of Pembroke college, and Mrs
Fox; two living witneſſes, that God can
at leaſt, if he does not always, give that
faith, whereof cometh ſalvation, in a
moment, as lightning falling from heaven."

The day from which Mr Weſley dates
his converſion, is May 24th, 1738.
He has introduced it with a ſtudied
ſolemnity, by an enumeration of the
various circumſtances we have recited,
with many more of the ſame ſort;
and it is immediately prefaced by an account of himſelf, from his infancy, till
that moment. It was on the evening of
this day, that he went to a ſociety in Al-
derſgate ſtreet, where ſome one was reading Luther's preface to the Epiſtle to the
Romans. About a quarter before nine,
ſays he, while he was deſcribing the
change that God works in the heart,

through faith in Chrift, " I felt my heart ftrangely warmed. I felt, I did truft in Chrift, Chrift alone for my falvation: and an affurance was given me, that he had taken away my fins, even mine, and faved me from the law of fin and death." He adds, that he immediately began to pray, particularly for his enemies and perfecutors, and declared to all that were prefent what he now felt. With fome intervals of doubt and fear, he continued in this fituation, and went up and down preaching and labouring with all his might.

Various were the effects of thofe peculiar doctrines, which Mr Wefley had preached for fome time before he profeffed to have experienced them himfelf. Many were offended, and among the reft, his brother Charles; who told him, he did not " know what mifchief he had done, by talking in this manner:" and

he obferves, that God did indeed from
that time " kindle a fire," which he hoped would never be extinguifhed. The
influence of this was fierce and decifive.
Many are reprefented as falling fuddenly
to the ground, in horror and agony not
to be conceived, and rifing again with
equal expreffions of peace and confola-
tion. Their converfions were ufually
attended with thefe violent fymptoms;
and, for feveral years, few meetings occurred, where Mr Wefley prefided, without one or more inftances of the fame
kind

It was not poffible, that fuch tranfactions fhould pafs without notice.
The confufion that too often prevailed,
the emotions of the perfons affected, and
the exultations of the reft, which were
feverely animadverted upon, gave great

and general offence. Many infifted, that
it muft either be occafioned by the heat
of the rooms and the agitation of the
animal fpirits, under difcourfes of the
moft alarming nature; or that it was
mere artifice and hypocrify.

As thefe objeftions were conftantly
urged, Mr Wefley has taken much pains
to refute them, producing in his journals an immenfe number of converfions,
attended with the fame fymptoms; and
fome, even of the objeftors themfelves;
who are faid to have fallen to the ground,
raving like the demoniacs in the Gof-
pels, and crying out, that it was "the
juft judgment of God for their wicked-
nefs and unbelief." Among others he
particularly inftances in a quaker, who
was much provoked with their diffimula-
tion. But he alfo "fuddenly dropt

down, as if thunderſtruck. The agony he was in, was terrible to behold.
We beſought God not to lay folly to
his charge. And he ſoon lifted up
his head, and cried, now I know, thou
art a prophet of the Lord." This happened while Mr Weſley was preaching
at Baldwin-ſtreet, where the cries of
the people were ſuch, that ſcarcely could
his voice be heard. The reader is referred, for further information, to the
firſt and ſecond journals. It may be
obſerved here, that Mr Charles Weſley's
objections to this new ſyſtem were gra-
dually removed. His converſion is dated from the 22d of May, 1738, two
days before that of his brother.

An account of their proceedings was
preſently tranſmitted to Tiverton, by a
Mrs Hutton of London, two of whoſe
ſons became converts to their opinions.

(215)

One of them is the perfon who is faid
to have been honoured fome time ago
with the notice of majefty. The lady,
who found herfelf not a little aggrieved, wrote to Mr Samuel Wefley, informing him, that his brother John was
become a wild enthufiaft or fanatic, and
was drawing her fons into the fame notions. She tells him, that fhe thought
him " not a quite right man," and begs
that when he fhould next come to his
houfe, he would " either confine or
convert him." She was particularly
difpleafed, that her fon was about to
publifh an abridgement Mr Wefley had
made of the life of Haliburton, a Scotch
prefbyterian. She had forbid him to
print it ; but obferves, that if his brothers
thought it would tend to the glory of God,
they would foon convince her fon, "that

O 4

God's glory was to be preferred to his. parent's commands."

Mr Wefley, in his lively manner, anfwered Mrs Hutton, by combating their opinions. He thought it not unlikely, that intenfenefs of thought and want of fleep might have difordered his brother. He treats their general fyftem as downright madnefs and delufion; and prays that God would "ftop the progrefs of this lunacy."

It was in the month of May that the firft methodift fociety was formed in London. Mr Wefley is particularly careful to diftinguifh the origin of methodifm into three diftinct periods. The firft commenced at Oxford, in 1729; the fecond at Savannah in 1736, when twenty or thirty met at his houfe; and the laft in London, on the firft of May, 1738, when " about fifty agreed to meet toge-

ther once a week, in order to a free converſation, begun and ended with ſinging
and prayer."

About this time his friend Böhler em
barked for America. On this occaſion
he contemplates, in a kind of rapture,
the happy effects of his arrival in
England , ſuch, ſays he, as will remain
" when the heavens and the earth paſs
away." Mr Weſley was now much
perplexed with doubts and fears, concerning his own ſtate, and determined to retire for ſome time to Germany ;
hoping that the converſation he would
meet with there, might be the means
of eſtabliſhing him more fully in the
faith. Taking leave of his mother, he
embarked on Tueſday, the 13th of June,
1738; and on Thurſday landed at Rot-
terdam. He arrived at Marienburn on
the 4th of July, and was introduced to

Count Zinzendorf. During his ſtay here
the Count took him to viſit the Count
de Solmes, where he " obſerved with
pleaſure the German frugality. Three
of the young counteſſes, who were grown
up, were dreſſed in linen; the count and
his ſon in plain cloth."

This obſervation reminds us of an anecdote we have heard of Mr Weſley, while
in Germany. It is well known, that one
of the firſt principles of moravianiſm, is
ſimplicity; or in other words, tractability;
a principle very proper to be inculcated
by the head of a party. One day, the
Count had ordered his pupil to go and
dig in the garden. When Mr Weſley
had been there ſome time, working in
his ſhirt, and in a high perſpiration, he
called upon him to get into a carriage
that was in waiting, to pay a viſit to a
German count : nor would he ſuffer him

either to wafh his hands or to put on his
coat. 'You muft be fimple, my brother,
was a full anfwer to all his remonftran-
ces; and away he went, like a crazed
man, in ftatû quo. This count we prefume, was the Count de Solmes. 'The
occafion of this extraordinary vifit, which
feems to have been intended merely as a
lecture on fimplicity, he has not taken
notice of : but of the authenticity of the
anecdote we have no doubt.

From Marienburn he went to Hernhuth. Here he found an American
acquaintance; and attending the con-
ferences and other meetings of the
brethren, had frequent opportunities of
hearing every thing explained, of which
he wifhed to be informed. Above all,
he was much comforted with regard
to his own ftate, by hearing it ftrongly
infifted upon, that the ftate of juftification

is perfectly confistent with doubts and fears; and that there is a diftinction between faith and the affurance of faith. This, if we underftand him right, was one prime object of his journey : and fuch, if we miftake not, was the doctrine inculcated by the brethren. As he has publifhed a particular account of the difcipline of the brethren,. we have no doubt, that he now looked forward, which he certainly did not in 1729, to his future labours in thefe kingdoms; and made himfelf immediately acquainted with their regulations, that he might form a code for his own focieties.

Of the conftitution of this church, it's officers, and it's difcipline, with the infinity of fprings and wheels in fo complex a fyftem, we fhall not fatigue the reader with the relation. Our averfion

to this fort of manœuvre in chriftian focieties, forbids us to enlarge on fuch a
fubject; and induces a wifh, that both
the Count, who was the projector, and
Mr Wefley, who too clofely imitated
him, had been more mindful of the
chriftian fimplicity.

END OF THE FIRST VOLUME.

For EU product safety concerns, contact us at Calle de José Abascal, 56–1°,
28003 Madrid, Spain or eugpsr@cambridge.org.